Steve Hedley

DERRY BOY

lola books

Printed in Spain by Safekat S.L., Madrid
ISBN 978-3-944203-70-6

Original edition 2024

CONTENTS

SYNOPSIS

I have been called "the most dangerous man in Britain" by right-wing commentators because of my political views. An uncompromising trade unionist and socialist, I acknowledged that our society was based on the exploitation of my class, the working-class. I did not start the class war which is as old as society itself but consciously took part in every battle and skirmish I could. Why would an Irish immigrant, whose people were brutalised and murdered by the British state, spend most of his life fighting for the working class in Britain? This book hopefully answers that question.

The book begins with one of my first memories, which was my Granny swearing during the Bloody Sunday massacre. It continues through my childhood where citizens of my hometown Derry, set up autonomous zones outside the control of the British state. I explain how my politics were formed by acts of barbarity from Britain including collusion with loyalist terrorists and allowing 10 young men to starve to death. I explain the effects that the heroism of the hunger strikers had on me and a generation of my peers and how this has shaped Irish politics ever since.

I trace my political development from meeting striking miners in Ireland to being forced to emigrate to England and taking part in momentous events there from opposition to the Poll tax and Iraq war, and resisting fascism on the streets, to becoming second in command of one of the most powerful trade unions in Britain the RMT. I explore the role of unions, their strengths and limitations and reach the conclusion that without conscious revolutionary leaderships, Unions with right wing or reformist leaderships only perpetuate the capitalist system and their leaders are indeed "the loyal lieutenants of capitalism".

I explain the consequences of being an effective trade unionist and how I was blacklisted, spending a year out of work because the bosses and political police (Special Demonstration Squad) conspired to keep me unemployed.

I explore some of the events and debates in the RMT union especially around the Covid period and after. The decisions taken by the leadership were in my view disastrous and have led the union on an increasingly right-wing trajectory, encapsulated by the entire union leadership crossing the picket line of a worker they had sacked.

Faced with climate catastrophe and war, both of which are inevitable parts of capitalist competition to capture markets and generate more profit from the exploitation of workers worldwide, I attempt an analysis of how catastrophe is imminent if we continue on our current path, and offer an alternative vision. I advocate a realignment of the left by abandoning identity politics and concentrating on issues that unite the working class such as economic beneficial, climate friendly jobs. Time is running out for great swathes of humanity; the working class and poor are suffering disproportionately from climate change and will pay with our lives if we don't force a change in policy. Finally, this book ends on a call to arms of all who are exploited by capitalism to come together and effect change, only we the working class have the material need to avoid millions of deaths, as they will be our deaths. Only we can be our own saviours, but time is short, and we need to act now.

FOREWORD

This book is a series of memories and reflections upon current events. Memories can change over time. It is not meant to, nor can it be a comprehensive account of all that has taken place in my lifetime. It is merely what has stuck in my mind and my attempted analysis of these events. I also needed to write down what I think some of the solutions may be, as I don't think that up until this point I have read anything most working-class people can relate to, and in my own small way I want to help remedy this. I have tried to be as honest as I could be about how I felt at different times in my life, and feelings also change over time, so if what I've written offends you, I can only say "get over yourself". As someone told me when I first criticised a union rep, if you think you can do better then throw your hat in the ring, so feel free to write your own account, offer your own solutions, it will most likely enrich the whole debate and if you can't do any better, you'll be comforted to know yow will struggle to do any worse. Finally, I must thank all my daughters and my ex-wife Julie for encouraging me to write this book and Iona Burnell Reilly for reading it and giving me some very good advice along the way. I hope you, the reader, are challenged by my writing, and hope that it causes you at least to think critically and question everything that you've been told.

DERRY BOY

1 BOGSIDE "BRED"

People were crowding into my Granny's hallway wearing handkerchiefs over their faces to protect from the CS gas which stung the eyes and choked every man, woman and child in the Bogside. I could smell the terror, people were screaming and panicking, crying uncontrollably and then the unimaginable happened and my Granny swore. Those words are seared into my mind "Jesus Christ, the bastards". I was gobsmacked: Granny Mc Laughlin never swore, she was always scolding people who swore, including my Granda who would push the envelope and say "buck" when he had the backing of a few Guinnesses. Granny was a staunch Catholic and had that old-school, working-class sense of respectability, demanding we all say the rosary every night and never ever swearing. This was strange indeed. The living room became packed as people gathered around the Radio Rentals black and white TV, jostling to get a view of the latest reports of the atrocity. It seemed every few minutes more people were being reported murdered by the British army as the world's media gathered in Derry that day to report on a civil rights march. The Brits couldn't cover this up like they had Ballymurphy or several other massacres of civilians; "Bloody Sunday" as it became known was broadcast across the world exposing the vicious brutality of the murderous British state for all to see. I was three and a half years old, and this was one of my earliest memories.

I lived in Creggan about ten minutes' walk from Granny's and already hated the Brits. They killed my budgie by firing

CS gas indiscriminately into the flats where we lived. In retrospect, their actions were pure counterproductive sadism, they achieved nothing but to engender more hatred. They stopped people in the street and humiliated them, sometimes beating them, sometimes arresting and torturing them for weeks and months at a time. Night-time raids were frequent as people were turfed out of bed in the early hours, their houses ransacked, furniture smashed, property stolen and if there were any young men in the house, arrests and subsequent beatings frequently took place. We hated them, the whole community hated them, and they hated us back.

Shortly after Bloody Sunday, we moved to Tyrconnell street two doors away from Granny's and with the other kids or wains as we were known I often stood guard at the barricade at the top of the street, which was meant to keep the army out of "Free Derry", the autonomous zone that had sprung up after the battle of the Bogside. When army Landrovers and pigs made incursions into our area we threw stones, bottles, and anything else we could get our hands on, this was often accompanied by the cacophony of women banging bin lids to alert IRA volunteers, who we idolised as our only protectors, that the Brits were about.

These were heady times, the Catholic population of the Bogside and the whole of the occupied six counties of Ireland had risen up after over forty years of oppression, discrimination in jobs, housing and even voting rights. Inspired by the Civil Rights movement in the United States, young activists like Bernadette Devlin and Eamonn McCann with their comrades in people's democracy had effectively broken the stranglehold of the ultra-conservative Nationalist party, with their brand of Marxism based on empowering the community and self-organisation. The orange state had reacted to peaceful protest by attempting to, quite literally, beat people into submission, with the sectarian police force and orange mobs setting upon the mainly student contingents: Mere girls and boys who dared protest institutional anti-Irish racism were beaten to a pulp.

It is worth giving a whistle stop tour of Irish history to understand how we got to this situation where Catholics and progressives were systemically discriminated against and beaten off the streets for the most reasonable demands. "British rights for British citizens", yes, seriously that was one of the demands of the Civil Rights movement.

Ireland's English problem began in the 12th century with the Norman Invasion, which initiated centuries of Irish resistance to rule from England and resulted in Irish rule throughout most of the country, except an area around Dublin known as the Pale. In 1541 Henry 8th declared himself King of Ireland. In order to maintain control, Henry initiated a plantation of English settlers in Irelands. Irish people were dispossessed of their lands, and this was given to the settlers.

King James 1st led a far larger plantation in Ulster, which was by far the most rebellious province, by bringing in thousands of Protestant settlers from Scotland and England between 1606 and 1609, forcefully taking the best land away from Catholics and giving it to the newcomers. This ensured that the settlers who had benefited by the immiseration of the native population, and divided from them by religious difference, would be loyal to the crown in order to maintain their stolen lands and privileges.

Resistance continued and Oliver Cromwell invaded Ireland between 1649 and 1651, driving Catholics out of Ulster, Munster and Leinster, and banishing them to Connaught on pain of death. "To hell or Connaught" was not a slogan but a terrifying reality for Irish Catholics. The Penal laws outlawed Catholic priests and clergy and forbade Catholics from higher education, professions and owning land. By 1778 Catholics held only around 5% of the land in Ireland.

In 1789, Theobald Wolfe Tone, one of the leaders of the United Irishmen, the fathers of Irish Republicanism, who were almost exclusively Protestant, led a rebellion to end British rule.

The Famine (1845–1851) saw the genocide of Irish people, mainly Catholics, with 2 million starving to death or forced to flee the country whilst the English were helping themselves to thousands of tonnes of Irish grain and massive amounts of cattle and other livestock. Various other rebellions took place, all unsuccessful, with Irish resistance vacillating between armed resistance and constitutional parliamentarianism.

The 1916 Easter Rising and the subsequent murder of its leaders saw nationalist sympathies multiply to such an extent that in 1918 Sinn Fein won the vast majority of parliamentary seats in Ireland. The years 1919 to 1921 saw the Irish Republican Army wage a War of Independence. This led to the Anglo-Irish treaty of 1921 which saw the Irish Free State emerge in 26 counties, while Northern opted out. The Free State became the Republic of Ireland in the 1940s and was formally recognized by the United Nations.

From its inception Northern Ireland was to be "a Protestant state for a Protestant people". Its institutionalized discrimination against Catholics, was designed deliberately and transparently to protect Protestant supremacy. The choice of a six county statelet with an inbuilt Protestant majority was meant to ensure unchallenged domination for generations. It also engendered a siege mentality where paranoia was fed to gain political advantage for ambitious politicians.

Easter 1966 was the 50th anniversary of the Easter Rising of 1916 which ultimately led to 26 counties of Ireland gaining their freedom from British rule. The commemorations were very much a peaceful affair celebrated with parades and marches. One exception was the blowing up of a statue of Admiral Nelson in Dublin. The IRA was in mothballs after a disastrous border campaign in the 1950s and posed no military threat to Britain. This did not prevent unionist paranoia growing, given voice by the demagogic Reverend Ian Paisley, a Protestant bigot who was virulently anti-Catholic. Paisley and other extremists set up the Ulster Constitution Defence Committee (UCDC) which had a paramilitary wing, the Ulster Protestant Volunteers (UPV), to defend Protestant supremacy.

Paisley distrusted the Northern Ireland Premier, Terrence O'Neill, whose views he deemed far too liberal. Paisley and his acolytes' wild rhetoric had really appalling consequences as a new Loyalist terrorist group styling itself as the Ulster Volunteer Force (UVF, after an organisation created in 1912 to oppose Home Rule) was founded in the staunchly loyalist Shankill road in Belfast. The UVF was led by Gusty Spence, an ex British soldier, and although it was relatively small, many of its members were also part of Paisley's UPV. The UVF unleashed a campaign of terror against Catholics, burning down houses, businesses, and even Catholic schools. A UVF petrol bomb attack killed an elderly Protestant lady, Matilda Gould. The terrorist attacks escalated with the murder of John Scullion, a Catholic who had no political connections. The murderous sectarian atrocities continued with three Catholics shot by the UVF as they came out of a pub, one of them, Peter Ward, being murdered in the process. The UVF were banned in Britain and Ireland after this cowardly murder.

At the same time the Northern Ireland Civil Rights Association were campaigning to end discrimination against Catholics in jobs, housing and voting and to reform the sectarian RUC, a police force that was less than 10% Catholic, and routinely brutalised the Catholic community using the Special Powers Act to jail people without crime or trial.

Protestant politicians explicitly wanted to preserve Protestant privilege and their paranoia was inflamed by NICRA who they saw as a Republican front. Some Republicans were NICRA members, but they were small numerically in the organisation and not influential in its decision making.

An important event occurred on 24th August 1968, when UPV members attacked a NICRA march from Coalisland that was attempting to go to Dungannon. Police watched on as marchers were badly beaten with cudgels by the loyalist thugs, this spectacle was to be repeated many more times that year. A Civil Rights march in Derry on 5th October, was banned by the government, and when protesters assembled anyway, the RUC beat them mercilessly with batons injuring 100 people which included many high-profile nationalist politicians. This was caught on camera, broadcast on the news, and sparked serious rioting in Derry.

Terrence O'Neill, in an effort to avert more trouble and sensing the very bad international publicity his government was getting, promised the Civil Rights movement concessions. On 1st January 1969, People's Democracy, a small Trotskyist organisation started a march from Belfast to Derry. When the demonstration got to Burntollet Bridge, loyalists, including some off-duty RUC men armed with iron bars, bricks, cudgels and bottles, launched a vicious attack. Despite being badly beaten the marchers continued to Derry where again they were attacked by loyalist thugs. The RUC then began a pogrom in Derry's Bogside attacking people indiscriminately and ransacking Catholic homes. The community defended itself, setting up defence committees, using petrol bombs and barricades to stop the police terrorising them and setting up "no go areas" where the forces of the state could not enter. Loyalists even bombed water and electricity plants in 1969, blaming the IRA and the Civil Rights movement, to get support for their own cause.

In April 1969, the Loyalists and police attacked civil rights marchers in Derry, and the RUC smashed into the house of Samuel Devenny beating him and his family, leaving his teenage daughter unconscious. Samuel died on 17th July from his injuries. On 13th July, RUC officers murdered another Catholic, Francis McCloskey, in Dungiven, beating him so badly that he died the next day.

The major clash, which was to have lasting repercussions began on 12th August, the battle of the Bogside lasted for three days when local youths fought off loyalist and paramilitary police attempts to launch another pogrom against the Catholic area. Triumphalist sectarian marching bands and their supporters backed by their brethren in the police were fought off by the heroic Derry people who defended their community. The police lost control of the situation and the Catholic community were victorious. Belfast and other Catholic areas began rioting in sympathy with Derry and to draw away the crown forces from the city. Loyalists responded by launching their own pogroms against Catholics in Belfast, burning down whole streets of Catholic houses. What remained of the IRA attempted to defend against the attacks with a few antique weapons. Police murdered a nine-year-old boy named Patrick Rooney, shooting him dead when they inevitably took the side of Protestant mobs against the Catholic victims.

Thing had gotten so serious that the 26-county Prime Minister, Jack Lynch, called for United Nations intervention, condemned RUC brutality, and set up a refugee camp just across the border from Derry in Donegal. He even threatened a humanitarian intervention using Irish troops if Catholics were left unprotected. The injuries of the state terror mounted, 10 people had been murdered, people had been killed, over 700 injured, including 154 by shooting. Hundreds of homes had been so badly damaged that they had to be demolished. 1,505 Catholic and 315 Protestant families were forced to leave their homes. The state responded by launching Operation Banner, sending in masses of British troops on 14–15th

August. These were initially welcomed by most nationalists, before they turned on the community and became another force to oppress Catholics. A barbed wire fence was constructed between the Protestant Shankhill and Catholic Falls areas of Belfast. This was to become the Peace Wall which still exists nearly 3 decades after the Good Friday agreement. Even the British state could not ignore the sectarian RUC's role in the riots. The Hunt committee eventually concluded that the RUC should be disarmed, and the B Specials abolished. The only policeman killed was shot by the loyalist UVF.

For a brief time, Derry's people ran their own affairs (1969-72). The police, the army and to some extent the state was forbidden to enter Catholic areas. Having failed to defeat the risen people in the Battle of the Bogside (12th-14th August 1969), when orange mobs celebrating the lifting of the siege of Derry attempted to conduct a pogrom in the Catholic Bogside area, and were supported in doing so by their brethren in the police and notoriously anti-Catholic B specials, the orange state had to concede defeat, at least temporarily. In the end the forces of the state were fought to a standstill by the local youth who poured petrol bombs, bricks, and rubble down on their heads from the commanding heights of Rossville flats.

Free Derry was world famous, and obviously the threat of good example could not be tolerated by the British state. I often wonder if the Brit government knew exactly what they were doing on Bloody Sunday, fully understanding that the cold-blooded murder of 14 civilians, and the shooting of 12 more who survived, would swell the ranks of the IRA, but knowing that ultimately any guerrilla army could not defeat the British state and its loyalist murder squads and would at some point seek compromise. This although a risky strategy for the Brit government, fraught with sectarian murder and near civil war, was none the less preferable to the Brits than a real revolutionary situation developing where citizens committees ran their own affairs. I mean if Derry could do it why not, Belfast, Glasgow, Liverpool, Birmingham, or Leeds? Yes, I'm suggesting that there was the real possibility of the government taking a decision that would instigate a 30-year sectarian bloodbath rather than leave the door open to any kind of socialist politics. The massacre itself was whitewashed for 30 years and the commanding officer responsible for this atrocity, Colonel Derek Wilford, was given an OBE.

Our street and indeed our house was a hotbed for debate. The IRA had split into two factions in 1969.The socialist, Official IRA, who in broad terms saw themselves as the defenders of the Irish working class and heirs to the 1916 Republic, and the Provisional IRA, who were much more nationalist and militarist and could be described as the defenders of Catholic communities. My family were initially very sympathetic to the officials or "stickies" as they were known (the name came from them selling Easter lilly badges with sticky backs as opposed to the Provo lilies which were held on with a pin). The overt Marxism of the officials did not play well with the Free State government, made up of Fianna Fail who shared their hatred of socialism with their even more conservative opposition, Fine Gael. The Irish American diaspora of course didn't much like reds either and wanted a bit of good old-fashioned militarist revenge, hence the massive funding for the Provos and the fact that the Officials scaled back and eventually abandoned their armed struggle, enabling the Provisionals to become the dominant force all over the occupied six counties within a few years.

The Brits made me an enemy for life when they personalised the conflict by shooting my pet border collie Terry, claiming that they thought he was a sniper and leaving him for dead in the lane a few doors above our house, nearly adding him to our own dead pet role of honour, headed by my gassed budgie. What had the bastards got against harmless animals? For good measure they had also nearly shot me and my brother Keith as we played cowboys in the lane a few months later; we were aged 4 and 2 respectively and, obviously part of the renowned and feared IRA midget brigade, armed with a wooden sticks, cowboy hats, and sheriff badges, we were legitimate targets in the well-trained eyes of the Brit occupiers. Me, Keith, later our cousin John and our friends Longo (John Long), Blackie (John Black), the Dohertys (Jackie and Martin), and the Dorans (Kieran and Gary) all played our part in fighting for Irish freedom by stoning the brits whenever they appeared, and calling them all sorts of swear words none of which any of us understood. I can honestly say we had no fear of the Brits, but were absolutely terrified of our mothers or "Mas" as we called them, finding out what we were up to, and were always wary of touts.

Our safe havens were Dorans, where rebel music was always on the record player, telling us of the heroes who had died for Ireland, and Longs, whose dad made ornaments from plaster moulds, and we would steal the paint and put it into bottles to throw at the crown forces. Green paint was our favourite, as we somehow believed that this would wind the Brits up more. We would hide in the grass in Celtic Park and hurl our paint bombs at the passing army vehicles shouting, "Up the Provos" and "Fuck off back to England". Now I'm not advocating a return to these activities, but all this rioting exercise meant that there was no child obesity crisis in the 1970s. Sometimes we'd even phone the police from a phone box just to throw things at them when they arrived, it's a wonder we weren't all shot.

It is crazy now to think that children born into conflict just regard it as normality. We all cheered on the IRA although we had no idea what the struggle was about except that we were the good guys, and the Brits were bad, as they had stolen our country. We all saw and heard bombs go off, participated in riots, sometimes for recreation, were stopped and searched on a daily basis at army check points if we wanted to go to school or the town centre. We all had our houses raided, had neighbours, friends and even family arrested and tortured for no reason, other than they were Catholic, and to us this was just the way the world was. It was a shock to me when I first visited England that people there had so much freedom compared to us, but later I was to learn that this in itself was somewhat illusory.

Keith and I attended St Eugene's school which rudely interrupted our patrolling of the street's barricade. The educational authorities were obviously aware of our revolutionary potential and decided to incarcerate us all day in the hands of the some of the most ruthless counter revolutionary elements in Ireland, the nuns. The school was run by nuns but also had civilian teachers who were equally classist, snobby and sadistic. I did well at school because the nuns at the orphanage where I was adopted blagged my adoptive parents that my dad was a doctor (it turned out he was a brickies labourer). Therefore, it was expected that I was going to be intelligent, was encouraged to be so and to a certain extent this became a self-fulfilling prophecy, all be it based on porkies told by nuns. My brother didn't have such a creative nun on hand to embellish his credentials and therefore the expectations of him were I think lower, which is a real pity as he's one of the smartest men I know.

Our activism wasn't completely dead: at weekends we would torment the "peace woman" a member of a group opposed to violence in our street by kicking her door and shouting "soldier doll" through her letterbox. My uncle who lived with Granny two doors away had nicknamed her Tonga, after the obese queen of Tonga, and this was quickly added to our repertoire of taunts. This all came to a sudden end when Ma was informed of our subterfuge, and we got battered senseless and threatened with a priest. To be fair the paedo scandal had not yet broken, but looking back that was a bloody sinister threat. I never forgave the peace people for my beating and now had proof of them being touts. When "Tonga's" car was torched, there was a debate if it was the IRA or an insurance job as the next one was far newer and smarter looking, my money was definitely on the latter.

My mum liked a drink, as did most of our family, and would be out to "Bingo" most nights, obviously getting lost along the way home and ending up in the pub for hours, coming home pissed. She and her smoking partner, my aunt Philomena, were liberated women before it came into vogue. I have a confession to make, and that terrible secret is that my adoptive dad was English, he was a complete bastard, and therefore was in no capacity a deterrent to my hatred for the other English bastards occupying our country. Why he tolerated Mum's behaviour was a mystery. He was ex-navy, an electrician by trade who ended up working for the Swilley buses as an engineer, until he had an accident and became disabled. All this drinking scandalised the ultra-Catholic neighbourhood that we lived in, and no doubt we were the butt of a lot of the gossip, deserved or undeserved. The fact that my adoptive Dad was English obviously raised suspicions although he always professed his "socialism" (in reality, Old Labour welfare capitalism) and his support for Irish independence. I think at least his labourism may have been genuine.

Kids in those days were numerous with families of six or more very common. This meant that each street had gangs of kids who would often fight with the next street along. Our main enemies were from Limewood street, the next street along from us, and battles would commence in the lane between the streets until someone was hit with a brick or an adult appeared and gave chase to us. Fights would take on added importance when the 15th of August, the anniversary of internment came around and each street would build a bonfire and other streets would attempt to steal it or "raid" it as we termed it back then. It's incredible to think now that adults encouraged and attended these bonfires usually stacked against the side of somebody's wall and full of tyres that gave off dense choking black smoke. Despite the obvious dangers, I would say my childhood was good, I was quite studious, enjoyed reading, especially Marvel comics, and as we had only two children in the household, we got lots of toys and new clothes, usually from Freeman's catalogue which my Dad ran until most of his customers knocked him. Despite several threatening letters from Freemans, they never did have the bottle to come into the Bogside and try to get their things back, which is just as well as their goods may well have been liberated and their van hijacked as an example to other capitalist predators.

We left the Bogside when I was about 10, lured by the promise of an inside bathroom in a new house in the Galliagh area about three miles from our previous abode. I remember the day we left, my Granny was distraught, it was as if we were emigrating to Australia rather than a 15-minute drive away. All the neighbours turned out to wave my Ma goodbye, some probably secretly relishing the fact that she'd fallen from grace in moving to a council house and away from their privately owned street. My Dad probably saw it as a chance to separate mum from the other drinkers and her partner in crime Philomena, in particular. As it turned out, this wasn't an altogether unsuccessful strategy as her drinking was largely restricted to the house from then on with just the occasional foray to "the Bingo" on special occasions.

2 PLANET OF THE IRPS

Having moved to Galliagh we settled in and made friends in our "square" which was how the houses were arranged. Our neighbours on one side were Sinn Feiners and on the other side, members of the IRSP (Irish Republican Socialist Party), who had split away from the Official IRA when the latter abandoned the armed struggle. This inevitably led to increased surveillance and raids on our house. Galliagh, for reasons of which I am unsure, had a large contingent of IRSP supporters, which led to detractors labelling it "planet of the irps" (pronounced Urps.) The next couple of years passed quietly as I completed my last two years of primary school and was recruited into being an altar boy at the local church, St Joseph's. I think Jesus must've been as surprised as I was at this turn of events, although he never mentioned his misgivings to me once. I went to the local Slievemore school, where my brother Keith was outclassing me in naughtiness, flooding the toilets and even being held captive in a police van after they caught him running away after he'd thrown a brick at it. This made him incredibly popular especially with girls just as I was developing into a boring goody goody swot.

Like most schools in Derry, my primary school was a Catholic school, and the children were exclusively from a Catholic background. Reflecting on this in later life I had grave concerns. Derry unlike Belfast had quite clear dividing lines, most areas by this time had either a vast majority of Catholic residents or a vast majority of Protestants. Galliagh was a Catholic area, so every child there was drawn from the surrounding area and was Catholic. In secondary education things were a bit different, the three main secondary schools were miles away from the districts where most pupils lived, and this forced a commute of around three miles every day. That said, the secondary schools were again exclusively Catholic, and this made no sense except to perpetuate the power and influence of the church. If people had to travel anyway then it would seem logical to have schools of mixed religion or of none. I don't want to exaggerate the potential effect that this would have had socially and politically, but I think mixing with kids from other religions would inevitably have led to friendships, which may have helped dispel myths and eventually have helped break down the sectarian divide. Most of my school mates would never have met a Protestant at school for their entire educational period and the same could be said for Protestant kids, who would never have met a Catholic. Even after nearly 30 years of the peace process, the divisions in education still remain. The main reason for sectarianism is the British occupation of the Northern six counties of Ireland, because the British nurtured and encouraged religious strife, in order to divide, conquer and rule the inhabitants of the North. If that division is to be broken down, however, a good starting place is the education system. The fact that this hasn't happened is partly because of the communitarian structure of politics in the North, where every major political party draws its support from either the Catholic or Protestant communities, so that it therefore in the parties' interests to maintain the segregation. *Only In 143 from I,000 schools in the North was there at least 10% of pupils from both*

Protestant and Catholic communities. 287 schools had either no Catholics or no Protestants.

Our house in Galliagh was opposite farmers' fields, which led onto a mountain trail in those days, and we spent the summer holidays either hiking for hours at a time or riding our bikes out early in the morning and returning about 9 or even 10 pm, as the daylight lasts longer in the North. We hung out with gangs of kids, often three or four from the same family, with the McDevits, Lynches, Wallaces and Hanleys, being our closest friends, but also with many other kids in the area too. This was before video games and fear of strangers limited the freedom of children.

I gained a scholarship to the local Grammar school, St Columb's college (or seminary for young priests, to give it its full title, I can only imagine that they called it that for tax reasons). I hated every minute I spent in that institution. They were on a mission to create a Catholic middle class and disliked working-class pupils interfering by gaining entry there. They discouraged pupils from mixing with kids from more working-class schools, even though in many cases pupils had siblings at these schools. I was a case in point, as my brother Keith went to St Peter's, a secondary school in the Cregan area. Most of the teachers at St Columb's were appalling, the majority hit the kids with leather straps for any perceived infringement, with the Latin teacher, McGinty, revelling in his sadism and simultaneously taking money from working-class people who couldn't afford it in his role as part shareholder in a bookies shop. Rumours of teachers abusing boys sexually were also rife, and at least two of those most suspected were dismissed from the school shortly after I was expelled, near the end of 5th year just before my "O" levels.

The school was split into two premises: the first two years were done in Bishop Street just above the Bogside, and the rest of the college was situated at Buncrana road a few hundred metres from Galliagh. It was during my first year at Saint Columb's that my politics began to develop. We were taught Irish history from a largely nationalist point of view, although Republicanism was frowned upon. We learnt of the heroes of the 1916 rebellion, albeit with the almost total exclusion of the man who would become my personal hero for life, James Connolly, whose deeds were deliberately relegated to a tiny paragraph, in order to downplay them. The priests and their lackeys found Pearse's blood sacrifice drenched in Catholic symbolism far more palatable than someone who not only wanted to change the colour of the flag but the whole social order in favour of the working-class. This attempted minimisation of Connolly only piqued my interest in the man the Brits found so dangerous that they had to strap him to a chair and murder him as he couldn't stand up from his wounds. Simultaneously the event with some of the most far-reaching consequences of my life was beginning to take place: a hunger strike against the criminalisation of political prisoners began, in which 10 young men were permitted to starve themselves to death by a callous murderous British state presided over, in my opinion, by a Prime Minister who was the personification of evil itself, Maggie Thatcher. In the 1980s, it was considered shameful for teenage boys to cry, but I and many others wept openly with rage, sorrow and helplessness as one hunger striker died after another while the Brits mocked and our world erupted and changed forever.

When Bobby Sands, who had been elected MP during his death fast, died there was a storm, the rain beat down torrentially. Whether this was a natural weather phenomenon or the heavens expressing their outrage was a matter for debate – what was irrefutable was the social and political storm that the death caused. Immediately marches of protest were convened and the most serious rioting since the battle of the Bogside took place in Derry. Thousands of petrol bombs were thrown at the police and army, hundreds of vehicles set on fire, dozens of shops either bombed or burned to the ground. These scenes were repeated throughout the occupied six counties in every nationalist and Republican working-class area. The lie that these men were common criminals was exposed by the bravest of deeds, by those who overcame every human instinct for survival and gave their lives in protest at being declared common criminals; no criminal ever has shown such courage and fortitude turning their very bodies into instruments of resistance against Britain and its entire imperial arsenal. We couldn't attend school for around a month as buses couldn't run for fear of being hijacked and burned. Then as comrade joined comrade in their death throes, the riots following each death subsided little by little, as it became obvious that Britain would allow ever more Irish patriots to die, seemingly oblivious to the horror, opprobrium, and outright disgust that people throughout the world felt towards the Thatcher government and by extension Britain itself.

During this time, I attended several hunger strike protests and played a minor part in the rioting that ensued, throwing stones and bottles at the enemy. I personally witnessed the Royal Ulster Constabulary (RUC) firing plastic bullets indiscriminately at children and teenagers this resulted in the deaths of young people and further enraged the Catholic population. Everyone I knew wanted to join the IRA or INLA (Irish National Liberation Army) to avenge the hunger strikers, but most of us were too young. Nevertheless, from that day forward I could never accept as legitimate any British rule in any part of Ireland and would tacitly support any means of removing it. One fairly comical aside was that a few teenage lads from my school, who I knew fairly well, were arrested for high-jacking vehicles and setting them alight. It seemed the creation of a Catholic middle-class was not as smooth a process as my school authorities may have imagined. One of the lads wouldn't say a word under interrogation, confessing afterwards that his mum had threatened to kick the shit out of him if he talked. The fear of trained British inquisitors paled into significance at the terror Irish mothers inspired, well done Missus M.

It was during the period of the hunger strike and the repercussions that resulted from it that I first started to really analyse how the media operated. I hate to break it to all you, English people, but the BBC has always been an arm of the state, which just about does enough in feigning impartiality to allow willing fools to ignore this fact. This manifested itself during the hunger strike as reports of rioting were deliberately played down, "moderate voices" given far more airtime than their support in the community merited, and those considered militants demonised. Many studies have shown how all the mainstream news channels gave far more attention to the killing of soldiers, policemen, prison officers and indeed any unionists than they did to the death of Catholics. We watched how the army and police murdered children with plastic bullets and how politicians of all persuasions in Britain condoned this, or at least acquiesced in it by their silence. We even had a ridiculous position where Sinn Fein representatives could not speak in the media, but could be filmed, and actors were employed to do voiceovers in the accents of those forbidden from talking. At the same time, the British state were running loyalist death squads, who were murdering innocent Catholics with impunity often guided by state agents and assets. The media of course gave this minimal coverage. This scepticism of the establishment's mouth pieces would stay with me for the rest of my life and would remain the filter through which I saw the world.

The hunger strike and its aftermath saw the rise of Sinn Féin as a political party. The adoption of "the ballot and the Armalite" strategy led them to take up council seats in the occupied six counties in the North of Ireland. In the Northern Ireland Assembly elections of 1982, Sinn Féin won 10 percent of the vote. This would remain the figure until after the ceasefire when the party grew exponentially and is currently the biggest party in the North.

In 1984, my narrow Republican view of the world was somewhat challenged when I met a striking miner who had come to Derry to raise funds. He was staying at my friend,

Frank Kelly's house, as Frank's mother, Theresa, was a member of the Workers Party (formerly official Sinn Fein) and a trade unionist. I talked with him about the strike as I had seen Arthur Scargill on the TV and couldn't fail to be impressed by Arthur's passion, wit, and intelligence. The miner explained how the strikers and their communities having been brutalised by the government, the police, and the bosses, were drawing parallels with the oppression of Irish people. They had even set up embryonic workers defence squads to protect against police attacks. This was encouraging for me as I began to consider the possibility that not all English people were bad after all.

Unfortunately, the miners were defeated as the ass lickers in the TUC didn't come to their aid, and the bosses funded a scab union, the UDM, to undermine the strike. Of course, once the UDM scabs had served their purpose, they were discarded and thrown onto the dole in the 1990s as Thatcher closed the vast majority of the remaining deep coal pits, with the industry being completely shut down by 2015. I couldn't help feeling that the scabs had gotten their just desserts and hopefully learnt a valuable lesson. The defeat of the miners set the working-class movement back decades, and exposed again the cowardice and incompetence of the TUC leadership and that of other trade union leaders. Rather than risk their big salaries and perks by doing what was necessary and calling strike action everywhere to support the miners, the bureaucrats scurried away in the face of the government-initiated attack on the entire working-class only to be picked off one at a time by a ruthless Thatcherite regime. A regime that was carrying out the wishes of its capitalist backers by breaking the power of the steel workers and others, and privatising public services to enrich the same capitalist class at the expense of the working-classes in Britain. Inequality was rampant, with the rich flaunting their wealth, while over three million languished jobless on the dole. What Thatcher and her backers did was unforgiveable, but what was worse was the absolute capitulation of the TUC and union leaderships. After all, we knew Thatcher and the Tories were our enemies, but the unions leaders were supposed to be on our side.

I will never forget the way the police on horseback charged the miners at Orgreave, beating them with batons. When the BBC showed this to the rest of Britain, and indeed the world, they deliberately switched the film reels to show footage of the miners retaliating which actually came after the police charged them first, so it looked like the miners had attacked the police. The BBC were doing what every working-class Irish Republican knew they would do, that is to cover up for the crimes of the British state, which after all they are an arm of.

3 DOING THE BOXER BEAT AND MEETING GIRLS

From early childhood, I had always been a boxing fan witnessing the historic battles of legends like Muhammad Ali, Joe Frazier, Ken Norton and George Foreman on TV. I absolutely idolised Roberto Duran who not only fought with a savage intensity, but also had vastly underestimated ring generalship and an amazing defence. I love watching or sometimes listening to local Derry hero, lightweight boxer, Charlie Nash, on TV and radio. It was no real surprise then that given the opportunity at the age of thirteen, I began attending a boxing gym, the Ring Amateur Boxing Club, with my brother and his friend David Nash who was the nephew of Charlie. Charlie Nash was a local celebrity, the former European lightweight champion and world title challenger. I wasn't a naturally gifted boxer, but worked very hard to improve my fitness and skills. I remember being beaten mercilessly by a lad half my size, Fergal O'Donnell, who would go on to win junior Ulster and Irish amateur titles, in my first sparring session. I was too stubborn to give up and eventually had 10 amateur fights, winning about half of them. I was privileged to be able to spar with Ulster champions like Paul Burke, Irish champion Roy Nash (nephew of Charlie), and many other really skilful boxers.

I was part of the club for about 5 years and occasionally would spar with Charlie Nash who would break my heart by standing right in front of me, bobbing and weaving so effectively that I could barely lay a glove on him. Charlie was an absolute gentleman who encouraged all the young boxers and never once lost his temper with any of us despite at times our own appalling behaviour. He was never big headed but very humble and always willing to give his time voluntarily to help us develop our skills. We would travel to fights all around Ireland in either Charlie's car or that of the other trainers, Tommy Donnelly and John Daley. It's wonderful to think how men like these all over Ireland, largely at their own expense, helped give lads a sporting outlet away from more dangerous situations that were taking place on the streets.

What I loved about boxing was the sense of camaraderie with the other fighters and the levels of fitness I achieved. The self-confidence and discipline that developed benefited me throughout my life and my love of boxing remains to this day. This is not to minimise the dangers inherent in the sport, and it might be controversial of me to say that I think many teenage boys want to fight – this may not sound politically correct but I believe it to be true, and this is better done in a controlled environment using boxing gloves and under the supervision of coaches, than in the street where no rules apply, and weapons abound. There is no feeling quite so good as winning a boxing contest; it is an amazing high that I've never been able to replicate in any other sport. On the flipside, if you lose a contest, you feel absolutely terrible. Having tasted victory and defeat, most boxers try their hardest to attain that high and avoid the low.

As my boxing training continued, and my body developed, I started to become attracted to girls and to my surprise some of them were even attracted to me. Having no sisters and having been banished to an all-boys secondary school, I was quite shy around girls who I regarded as an unknown and somewhat exotic entity. I met my first real girlfriend when I was 14, her name was Karen, and I became absolutely besotted with her. Unfortunately, her dad, who was huge, was not at all besotted with me and after several threats to make me stay away failed to deter me, he confronted me outside one of her friends' houses. This resulted in me punching him, and him grabbing me by the throat, until the house holders intervened and separated us. Karen, no doubt flattered by the attention, the star of her own little drama with two men fighting over her, used to sneak out of the house when she could to meet me, but after about a year the relationship petered out.

It was through Karen's sister that I met my future wife, Julie McColgan. Julie was a bit older than me which meant that she was a year ahead in school. Although I was very attracted to her, I never thought that anything would come of it, as girls usually went out with boys who were a few years older than themselves. Julie was the most beautiful creature I'd ever seen, as tall as me at that time, she had amazing blonde hair, the figure of a model, and the face of an angel. Despite being clever and funny, she was really down to earth and easy to talk to. She was utterly charming and a gifted amateur actress. Julie ended up asking me to go out with her which astonished me, and I quickly accepted. She became my first true love and would become my wife and constant companion for the next 14 years, before my single-minded selfishness and tunnel vision helped to destroy the relationship.

Julie left school at 16 and went to work at a shirt factory, at that time the major employers in Derry. This was bittersweet as she was very intelligent and would in later life go on to do a degree and work in midwifery in the NHS, but at that time she saw no further point in education. Likewise, I had been an insufferable rebel at school from about the age of 14, kicking back against the strict authoritarian regime of St Columb's. My form class 4, and later 5F, were notorious for unruly be-haviour, and would enact childish feats of rebellion like kick-ing over plant pots on the stairwells, kicking classroom doors and running off and even setting fire to bins and smashing fire alarms to get out of lessons. I would regularly backchat teachers if they tried to discipline me, and refused point-blank to allow them to use the leather strap on me. When one teacher grabbed me by the ear, I pushed him away, squared up to him and luckily, he thought better of it before the situation escalated. I was only about eight and a half stone but was as fit as a fiddle and could probably have taken on most of the teachers physically.

Eventually the school had enough of me, I was becoming increasingly rebellious, and the authoritarian middle-class regime exacerbated my need to kick back. By this point, I was not prepared to be talked down and controlled by peo-ple I had absolutely no respect for, as, I reasoned, they had no respect for my class. Eventually I was expelled, actually for something a friend of mine had done, which was to shout abuse at a teacher. I obviously refused to grass, and he refused to confess, though to be fair I might have done the same if I was in his position. Given my irreconcilable differences with the school regime and my previous history, I couldn't really complain. The expulsion was a few months before my "O" levels, and I ended up doing them in the city's all-girl grammar school, Thornhill, which was to become famous as it featured in the series "Derry Girls". At all times whilst at Thornhill, I was escorted around by two huge nuns, I wasn't sure if this was to protect me from the hordes of girls starved of male company, or to stop me impregnating them on the tea break. Anyway, my minders did a wonderful job as both me and the girls emerged completely unscathed. Somehow, I managed to pass all my exams with reasonable grades, so please accept a big belated thank you, Sisters.

Julie getting a job meant that she had money, and I didn't, and this led to me leaving home to get my own income. Julie had fairly strict parents and often clashed with her mother Hilda, who I was to become great friends with later in life, but didn't much like at the time. Her Dad, Matt, a nice man, with a very dry sense of humour, was like a peacekeeper between them on occasions. The clashes escalated until Julie left home and moved in briefly with my parents before we decided to squat in an unoccupied local flat. We stayed there for a few weeks before being evicted, with me becoming effectively homeless and ending up in a bed and breakfast, and Julie having to return home to her parents for a time until I got a council flat.

It was around this time that we learnt that we were to become parents. I attended the local technical college for a time studying "A" levels, but the lack of money and motivation led me to drop out and search, unsuccessfully as it turned out, for a job. We moved into my flat together in the Shantallow area and awaited the birth of our first child. Carlene Stephanie Hedley, as impatient as ever, arrived three months early on the 19th February 1986, weighing in at 2 pounds 12 ounces. She was immediately rushed to the Royal hospital in Belfast due to the lack of premature baby facilities in Derry. Amazingly she thrived and is currently a mother herself to son Cree and a property tycoon (I know I have no idea where I went wrong, as she just wouldn't buy the whole socialism thing). After moving to a three-bedroom house in Galliagh, I married Julie a month after my 18th birthday. I had no idea what marriage really was, nor of the role a husband should play to make such a sacrament successful, and this would have consequences down the line. The night before, me and my friends had got very drunk and a mass brawl ensued. More than one wedding guest turned up with black eyes.

I spent about 8 months on the dole in Derry or the "Brew" as it was called there. It was really a hopeless existence, with no money to spare or to treat my family in any way. I was applying for all sorts of jobs, but couldn't even get an interview for most of them. It came to a point where I was sleeping until nearly noon and staying up late at night, things had to change. Most of the young men and many young women were forced to emigrate to England, America, Australia and Canada, and other far-flung locations around the globe. I really didn't want to uproot my life especially with a baby girl and a new house, but there was little alternative. Not being able to secure work in Derry, I took Norman Tebbit's advice and "got on my bike". The journey took me to England to look for a job, leaving my little family behind for a time.

4 LONDON CALLING

I first arrived in London at the age of 18, having travelled by the cheapest way possible, a coach from Foyle Street and the Larne to Stranraer ferry. I was to stay in Kilburn at the Irish hostel in Quex road with about 100 other lads from all parts of Ireland, North and South. Another Derry fellah, Danny Toland, was already there, and we got a few weeks work with Murphys digging the roads. This was absolutely backbreaking work and neither of us stuck it out very long. I have to admit that the English were a lot nicer now that I'd stopped throwing things at them, and I even became friendly with some of them. Me and Danny pissed what money we earned away at Biddy Mulligans and the National dance hall. I was applying for all sorts of jobs when I was there but wasn't successful, so ended up going back to Derry for a couple of months.

Ironically, I was then given a start and returned to London. When I got off the coach in Victoria, I had the strangest of feelings like I had somehow come home. This was weird as I had only spent about two months in the capital and why I felt a sense of familiarity and almost welcome when I came back was simply inexplicable. I initially stayed with relatives and then got a private flat. Council housing was unavailable as I was told I'd made myself intentionally homeless even though I'd moved to London to take up a job offer. As usual Tory rhetoric about getting on your bike was completely divorced from the practical realities that working-class people faced. Julie and Carlene joined me after a couple of months, which looking back on it was probably a very traumatic experience for a new mother separated from her support network, and virtually friendless in a foreboding capital city. Needless to say, all of this was lost on me at the time.

We soon decided to squat into a housing association flat, aided and abetted by some local kids who helped us carry the furniture to our new abode. This lasted for over six months before we were again evicted and forced to separate, with Julie in a bed and breakfast paid for by the council, and me in a rented room until Julie was allocated a temporary council place in Plaistow, which led to a permanent council house in Canning Town. Canning Town was at the time very white and very racist, but many people had Irish parents or grandparents, so we had no real hostility and Julie settled well, making lots of friends there.

A couple of months before my nineteenth birthday I got a job on the railway at London Euston. It was there that I met the Local NUR union rep, Mick Ryan, who was absolutely inspirational, and I joined the union because of him. The rate of pay was appalling, but we pretended to work, booking massive amounts of overtime much of which we actually spent in pubs, and this fictitious overtime was enough to get by on. Mick was always haranguing us to attend union meetings, and me and another new starter, Gary Sculfor, eventually succumbed to going to the Jolly Gardeners, getting astonishingly drunk and abusing ASLEF drivers through an open window, even throwing beer at them when they had the audacity to retaliate. This somewhat inauspicious start to my trade union membership quickly improved when I met my childhood hero, Arthur Scargill, at an NUR picket at King's Cross station, which he off course refused to cross. The night before, we had slept at the union headquarters, (me, Donald Nicholson and Sean Kenny volunteered for the early picket) then on the Euston Road, as there were no trains in the morning due to the strike. We completely abused this hospitality, drinking all the miniatures we could find in the building (it was coincidentally my introduction to Glenfiddich), and telling the union officer Phil McGarry to "fuck off" when he tried to intervene and stop us singing rebel songs. Miraculously, we were still up at five for the picket and were photographed with Arthur with pictures appearing in the Evening Standard and most of the tabloid rags, next to articles totally misrepresenting the reasons for the action and demonising the union.

My drinking ability and total lack of decorum obviously impressed the union hierarchy when Mick was elected to a higher union negotiating body, sectional council, and this left a vacancy which I was encouraged to fill as a local rep. Mick had inadvertently spurred my interest when I complained about the lack of militancy in the union by saying, "if you think you can do better then put yourself forward". I took him at his word, so really all the subsequent chaos is really his fault, whereas I'm happy to take credit for the successful bits.

A huge formative experience for me politically occurred around this time, and took place when the poll tax demonstration was attacked by the police. This took place on 31st March 1990. People had gathered from throughout Britain to protest against the abolition of the rates system (in which people paid money to the council depending on the value of their properties, i.e. higher valued properties paid more) and its replacement with a system called the Community Charge where ever adult had to pay the same regardless of property value or earnings. There were about a quarter of a million people on the march which began at Kennington Park at about 1:30 pm.

We arrived at Trafalgar Square about an hour later, at this time there was absolutely no trouble, but ominously police began blocking roads around Whitehall and Downing Street causing bottle necks. The police started to throw their weight around harassing protesters, pushing and shoving them. Then police on horseback appeared and began to push into the protesters all along Whitehall, forcing the protest up towards Downing Street. I was sensing a trap and spoke to a couple of people that I was with, arguing that we should get out as it made no sense to herd us toward Downing Street, unless they planned to attack us there or to provoke trouble. It was one thing rioting in your local neighbourhood where you knew the territory and had prepared defences, but a completely different scenario being provoked and attacked by the police in central London, while all the time being filmed and probably then subsequently arrested.

Some of the people around us began sitting down in the road to peacefully protest and were dragged away and arrested for "obstruction". The mounted police then moved into the crowd forcing people into Trafalgar Square. At just after four o'clock, riot police charged the crowd in Trafalgar Square and about half an hour later riot vans began driving directly into the peaceful demonstration. People now began to react, throwing placards and sticks at the police vans. This may have looked bad on TV, but as rioting went was completely ineffective. Many people were simply trying to get back to their coaches which had come from all over Britain and were parked on the south bank of the Thames. These people in the main just wanted to get out of any strife, but were prevented from going by the police who blocked their way, battening people for no good reason.

By about 5 o'clock people had had enough of the police violence and began to react in a serious way, climbing scaffolds and throwing bricks and scaffold poles down at the police. Somebody then began to burn the builder's cabins and there was also a fire in the South African Embassy. For the next couple of hours, the police pushed people away from Trafalgar Square towards the West End, where windows were smashed, and some shops looted. I managed to get away from the madness around seven o clock when I got through police lines and walked to Kings Cross, where I caught a tube home.

Predictably the Labour party and even the Militant Tendency condemned the "rioters" and not the police, threatening to "hold an enquiry and name names". These so-called revolutionaries were prepared to grass people up to the police. On the other hand, the Socialist Workers Party and George Galloway put the blame where it belonged – firmly on the police and not those forced to defend themselves.

The poll tax riot was to be the beginning of the end of the Thatcher government. The tax itself was hugely unpopular, and the threat of disorder panicked the ruling class who no doubt started manoeuvring with their men in grey suits to find Maggie's successor. In November 1990, at the Conservative party's leadership contest, Thatcher didn't get a majority of votes. She subsequently withdrew her nomination, and this led to Chancellor John Major succeeding her as the Conservative leader. On 22nd November, Thatcher resigned and Major was elected. She was rewarded for her services to Capitalism and its ruling elite by being given a seat in the House of Lords as a Baroness. Margaret Thatcher was sadly missed by some, especially in Brighton, but most working-class people were delighted to see the back of her and the horrendous neo-liberal anti-working class politics that she became the figurehead for.

This whole process showed me that politics often took place on the streets and not in parliament. The left-wing of the establishment, the Labour party, the vast majority of trade union leaders and even some so-called Trotskyists, sided with the state against the oppressed when push came to shove. They proffered illusory solutions like waiting for a Labour government, or walking harmlessly from point A to point B listening to some boring speeches and then going home. Those who defended themselves from the police on the poll tax demonstration showed that there was a way to force change that short-circuited the longwinded and ineffective "democratic process". Bourgeois democracy as I saw it was a scam, where occasionally a right-wing Labour government would be elected to replace the Tories. Having gained power, Labour would change very little for workers and allow the rich to keep their wealth, influence and power virtually unaltered.

People taking to the streets and demanding change had sent such shockwaves through the system that the ruling class in Britain were forced to act almost immediately, fearing the potential rise in consciousness of millions of workers which threatened the power and extreme wealth of the elite.

5 I'M A UNION MAN I'M PROUD OF WHAT I AM

The NUR, National Union of Railwaymen (the forerunner of the RMT) was led at the time by Jimmy Knapp, a big gruff Scotsman, whose hair seemed to be shaped into horns at the side of his head. Jimmy had been elected on a left-wing ticket, but like many before him, the position of General Secretary and the union bureaucracy had pulled him into a more centrist position, much to the disgust of the organised left. Jimmy was a powerful speaker who could hold a room and inspire people. He led the NUR into a merger with the National Union of Seamen (NUS) in 1990 to form the RMT, which was to become one of the most powerful, militant, and high-profile unions in Britain.

Having been a local rep for a while, I started attending branch meetings regularly and then regional meetings once every two months. It was there that I met Sam Wallace. An old campaigner and socialist stalwart, Sam took me under his wing and was always available if I sought advice. He and Donegal man, Bill Kerrigan, used to play good cop/bad cop with the management, where Kerrigan would lose his temper or pretend to, it was really hard to tell the difference – sometimes threatening to throw managers out of windows – and then Sam would step in as the voice of reason and allow the grateful manager to do a deal that benefited the workers.

Sam introduced me to executive members in the union and encouraged us to organise mass meetings to build a head of steam for disputes. It was at one of these meetings in Aloysius Hall, Sommers Town, that I met one of the greatest trade unionists of his generation, Bob Crow. Bob had just been elected to represent London underground on the national executive, he was a big man with shoulder length curly hair at the time, and when he began to speak, it was like I'd been hit with a lightning bolt. I wasn't the only one. As I looked around, I saw the whole hall entranced and energised by what Bob had to say. He had the knack of explaining quite complex socialist ideas in terms that working-class people understood, and did so in an entertaining and humorous way. Bob was a proud Millwall fan, which just goes to show nobody's perfect. He was absolutely fearless and tore into not just the bosses, but the capitalist system, that by its very nature ran on impoverishing and exploiting workers, and he did it in a way that we knew exactly what he meant. When he was finished, he received a rapturous standing ovation, and I guess looking back I recognised greatness and supported him from that day onwards in his bid to become Assistant General Secretary, defend that position when challenged by right winger and darling of the TUC, Mick Cash, and subsequently in his successful bid to become General Secretary of the union.

In 1991, my shift pattern allowed me to go back to my local Further Education college, Newham, where over the next couple of years I did "A" levels but received far more valuable education from a lecturer who was an anarchist there, a guy called John Batt. John had good debating skills and was able to expose the limitations of left-wing Republicanism and labourite theory. I was impressed, as I knew there was truth in what he said about the horrors of capitalism and the absolute inadequacy of parliamentary means to remedy this. I went to an Anarchist bookshop, "Freedom books", in Whitechapel and tried to find out more, even attending some meeting before I became aware of the deficiencies in Anarchist theory, like recognising no democracy at all and the inevitable unelected hierarchy that develop when there are no democratic processes. It was, however, great to come across fresh ideas.

I was the local rep at Euston for about eight years; these were tumultuous times. There were not many strikes in this period and heart-breakingly for me, we did not even ballot to prevent the disastrous privatisation of British Rail, which began in 1994 and was complete by 1997. To strike may have risked the unions assets had the courts declared it illegal to ballot and strike on the issue, but this was never even put to the test. The unwillingness of the trade union bureaucrats to break the anti-union laws, putting their own privileged existence before what needs to be done to win is endemic in Britain's unions. The misleaders attempt to mask their treachery by pretending that they are concerned about "the members money" being sequestrated by the courts. In reality, most members never receive a penny from the unions, and the bureaucrat sits in a well-paid job, with a company car, a credit card and a good pension scheme that he is just not prepared to gamble with. Until the grass roots exert democratic control and seize power from the bureaucracy, industrial defeats are inevitable.

I think I was initially attracted to union and left-wing politics in general, as I saw it as an extension of the resistance that was going on against the British state's occupation of Ireland. The same ruling class were oppressing the Irish and British workers, so it was in my own interests as a working-class man and Irish Republican to do whatever I could to further the cause of the workers and the Socialist Irish Republic that I dreamed of. I tried to put myself heart and soul into any struggle that occurred, and the strikes that did occur were quite important ones. In 1989 after six days of action, we achieved an inflation busting 8.8 percent basic pay deal with add-ons that brought it to about 10 percent. This was in the teeth of fierce opposition from the Thatcher government. I had the added bonus of meeting my boyhood hero, miner's leader Arthur Scargill, on one of my first pickets.

The signallers strike in 1994 turned out to be the most important large-scale victory for trade unionists since the disastrous defeat of the miners a decade earlier. Signallers control the movement of trains, and therefore have massive industrial strength – if no signallers come to work, then no trains run, end of. This made the dispute very prominent in the public consciousness. There were only 4,600 signallers and the government could easily have negotiated a solution relatively cheaply. Instead, they tried to smash the strike as an example to other workers who might have been considering action. What a massive mistake that was, the signalling staff's tactics consisted of calling a series of 24- or 48-hour strikes, repeatedly shutting down the vast majority of the Rail Network. They were sustained by the rest of the union who contributed to the strike fund and the wider movement who donated generously to help win a pivotal dispute. This led to Railtrack manager, Robert Horton, threatening to sack the workers en masse, and only to rehire them if they abandoned striking. The workers held their nerve and after dozens of strike days, Railtrack and their government masters were forced to compromise by hammering out a deal at ACAS. The government climbdown was of course completely the opposite of what they intended and encouraged other workers to fight for deals that kept pace with inflation. As Bob Crow often said, "fear can be contagious, but courage can be even more contagious", and the whole movement took courage from our victory.

6 LEFT FIELD OR LEFT OUT?

During the signallers strike I was transformed from a rep into an activist. In order to raise money for the strikers, I was invited into workplace after workplace in London and sometimes further afield to speak at meetings explaining the signaller's case and collecting money for them. This was the first time I came into contact with the British left, and quite honestly, I was shocked. In Ireland virtually everyone I met who was a socialist or republican was working-class, the opposite was the case in London. The left seemed quite homogenous, drawn almost exclusively from the lower middle-classes who would talk in Marxist terms few workers could understand. They also dressed very bizarrely, and shockingly for so-called socialists, were very reluctant to buy a round in the pub after a meeting. They were good-hearted people by and large and they got us into workplaces to raise money, but they wouldn't last five minutes on a council estate, especially if they started ranting and preaching at people which they often did. I could really imagine workers being actively deterred from participating in socialist politics by this lot, probably reasoning "if these people are socialists, I must be something else". It was telling that most of them even talked about the working-class in the third person, tacitly acknowledging that they were neither culturally, nor even in reality, politically part of our class.

I had just about written the British left off as a load of middle-class quacks when I met a very different variety of leftie indeed. In the early nineties, the fascist BNP were gaining electoral support with their "rights for whites" slogans playing on the lack of resources in working-class communities and the dearth of council houses, and using this very effectively to sew division amongst workers on racial grounds. The abandonment and alienation of the working-class, and white workers in particular by the Labour party and much of the so-called left, meant that there was space for the fascists to organise in communities. The BNP and fascists generally always have strategies of controlling the streets. What this meant was that fascist thugs would physically attack left-wing paper sales, disrupt meetings, and try to intimidate their political opponents into avoiding going near places where the fascists were carrying out political work, giving the fascists a free hand to organise unopposed. Something needed to be done to remedy this situation and a group named Anti-Fascist Action picked up the gauntlet, determined to give the fascists a taste of their own medicine.

AFA was made up of Socialist Republicans in Red Action, Anarchists from the Direct-Action Movement (DAM) and various small Trotskyite sects together with individual anti-fascists. There was a clear agenda to defend left-wing spaces and to carry the battle to the enemy by disrupting their activities. As a young man, I was far more suited to this style of politics than listening to boring, patronising speeches from posh people. I joined AFA after they helped defend a "Troops out" march from hundreds of fascists who hooked up with football hooligans trying to attack it. We were physically attacked outside a pub in North London, getting pelted with bottles and bricks, then charged by a large crowd of Nazis. Being hugely outnumbered we had to retreat inside the pub where one comrade, Carl, hid behind the door armed with a crate of bottles waiting for fascists to come in, then jumping out and smashing the bottles over their heads. Like a scene in a comedy, Carl repeated this manoeuvre at least four times and the enemy continued to be caught unawares each time. Although my adrenaline was pumping, I couldn't help but laugh at his audacity and their stupidity. Despite being badly outnumbered, we held our ground and made our opponents retreat, many of them obviously 'fell over' in their haste to escape and had to avail themselves of that paragon of socialism, the NHS, in the form of the Accident and Emergency department to treat their injuries. At last, I had found some working-class political people outside of the union and on the left who I could relate to.

Over the next few years, this pattern of confronting Fascism was repeated in one form or another all over England, Scotland and Wales. To counter the right-wing influence in football, AFA organised on the terraces. Celtic, Hibbs Wrexham, Liverpool and Manchester United became anti-fascist fortresses, with Aston villa activists overcoming fascist sympathisers in their own support, and keeping the fascists in check there too. This was not achieved by student union type debate, typical of the majority of the left, but by confronting the fascists ideologically, and physically when necessary. Fanzines such as TAL at Celtic and Red attitude at Manchester United pushed anti-fascist and socialist ideas in a form palatable to football fans, using humour and working-class knowhow to win people over. If all else failed, I would imagine, in the words of singer Kieran Murphy in his song about racists, people may have been told "if you keep it up and you're going to get a slap". Of course this is conjecture as I never actually witnessed it, honest.

A major pitched battle occurred between the forces of the left and the right on 12th September 1992. Anti-Fascist Action fought neo-Nazis heading to a Blood & Honour Nazi music gig in what was to become known as "the Battle of Waterloo", as it occurred in and around London's Waterloo railway station. There were thousands of combatants on each side. We arrived early and occupied the fascist re-direction point where Nazis would be told the location of their planned gig. As the fascists arrived, they were given "stern talkings to" with many going home to lick their wounds. Later, neo-Nazis began arriving en mass, some wearing swastikas. Anti-fascists were forced to vigorously defend themselves and managed to chase the Nazis all around the station area, forcing them to abandon their planned music event. Me and a couple of mates, having just had to defend ourselves against some skinheads, were resting outside a restaurant when the doors flew open and a mob of skinheads charged towards us. I remember thinking "we're fucked now" as there were at least fifty of them. Having no chance of outrunning the mob, I started throwing punches in desperation, but to my astonishment, rather than attack us they ran straight past. It turned out that about ten Nazi skins were being chased by a larger group of anti-fascist skinheads who caught up with them and attempted to gently persuade them of the error of their ways. These events at Waterloo were a clear victory for militant anti-fascism, and a notice of intent that London would not tolerate fascists gathering there.

In 1993, Derek Beacon of the fascist British National party was elected in Millwall. This electoral success was not isolated, and at its zenith, the BNP had 50 local Municipal Council seats, various Parish Council seats, and a London Assembly member in 2008. Incredibly, they gained almost a million votes in the Euro elections of 2009. This electoral support quickly declined as internal splits and money issues weakened the Fascist party massively.

The BNP had opened an office, their headquarters, in a bookshop in Wickham Lane in Welling, Southeast London, in 1989. The local area almost immediately witnessed a big increase in the number of racist attacks, and this pattern continued over the next few years, including the racist murder of a young Black man, Stephen Lawrence, in 1993.

The BNP bookshop was an affront to ethnic minorities, the left, and I would argue, all decent people. On 16th October 1993, 30,000 anti-fascist demonstrators gathered to march on the bookshop to demand its closure. I was one of them. AFA had not mobilised for the day, seeing it as a sting operation where the police would cause a confrontation, and then arrest activists when the inevitable response came. As it turned out, the AFA analysis was not far off the mark. The police blocked the route, and we avoided them by changing directions, avoiding any confrontation with them, and heading towards Welling. Up to this point, the march was passing off peacefully, but as we approached the bookshop, police in riot gear blocked us. They had set up an exclusion zone around the bookshop. Then the riot police, supported by loads of mounted police, started pushing us away from the bookshop in a very aggressive and uncalled-for way. When people resisted, the police baton-charged us, smashing the lead steward Julie Waterstone of the Anti-Nazi League over the head, and leaving blood streaming down her face. The clashes went on for about two hours with masses of riot police attacking the march until they cleared us away from the shop, effectively protecting the fascists. Over 60 protesters were injured together with 12 coppers, who also got hurt. The cops also arrested Duane Brooks, who had been with Stephen Lawrence when he was murdered, and spent over a million pounds to protect the fascist headquarters. The bookshop was finally closed in 1995 by the local council. It says something about the state of a police force when a young man traumatised by his friend's racist murder is arrested and harassed, but the hate preachers of the BNP, whose presence led to a massive spike in racist attacks, enjoyed police protection.

Despite this set-back for anti-fascists, the BNP were forced to abandon their policy of controlling the streets, as AFA made those streets very unsafe for fascists indeed. This led to a 1994 statement from the BNP leadership that there would be "no more marches, meetings, punch-ups".

Although the BNP was forced to abandon their strategy of dominating working-class spaces, smaller groups like the National Front and the openly Nazi Combat 18, were still attacking leftists. AFA stewarding groups again met fire with fire, and after several "vigorous debates" C18 disintegrated due to squabbles over money and drugs, with rivals literally murdering each other for the spoils. My participation in AFA remains one of my proudest and most worthwhile achievements, and

I will always believe that the organised working-class need to crush fascist organisations before they crush us. Anti-racism and anti-fascism are not about charity or even solely solidarity. Fascists demonise minorities in order to split the working-class. They are no more than puppets and lackeys for the super-rich, who do not want even the vestiges of bourgeois democracy to interfere with their profit-making and the power this gives them. When fascists come to power, they do not stop at attacking minorities, but inevitably turn on the trade unions and anyone who opposes the ruling elite; therefore, Fascism has always been and always will be our deadliest enemy as a class, and can be shown no quarter whatsoever. Congratulations to Gary, Andy, Stevie Tal, Tommo, Tony, Duncan, Brad and all the other heroes, too numerous to name, who helped to stem the rising Fascist tide at this dangerous time.

7 STEVIE USED TO WORK ON THE TRAINS

By the late 1990s, the RMT was being transformed into one of the most militant and powerful unions in Britain. Bob Crow had been elected as Assistant General Secretary as the left candidate, and had beaten off a subsequent challenge by the right-wing candidate, Mick Cash, who is on record as describing London underground workers and RMT members as being like "drunks on a Saturday night, willing to fight anyone, anytime, anywhere". This anti-worker rubbish may have played out well in the ivory towers of the Labour party and TUC, but rallied support for Bob within the union, and he beat Cash at the ballot box. Cash did subsequently get elected as Assistant General Secretary, and then unfortunately went on to succeed Bob as General Secretary before his, in my opinion, disastrous right-leaning leadership led to him into conflict with his own executive, and his subsequent retirement due to mental health issues, and not getting his own way on my appeal. Bob was touring the country, preaching trade union values and Socialism, and in doing so, building not only his own base, but inspiring like-minded people to become active.

The breakup of British Rail and the appearance of private profit-making companies in the railway was terrible for the British public, in terms of the prices they would pay for tickets, the appalling safety record that would ensue, and the shocking service they would receive; however, it did present opportunities for the union. Where previously the government dictated what pay terms and conditions workers would receive, privatisation meant that this would now be devolved to the private companies (there was still obviously influence and pressure exerted by governments behind the scenes). Hitting private companies in the pocket was to prove a far more effective strategy than sitting in endless meetings with British Rail management, and union leaders repeating the ridiculous mantra that going on strike would stop the election of a Labour government. Such a government, the bureaucrats told us, would be the messiahs not just us, but the entire working class. Yeah really, this is the shite, trade union leaders spouted to defuse disputes and potential disputes, despite the overwhelming mountain of historical evidence which showed the exact opposite.

Euston, where I worked, and where West Coast mainline ran all the way to Scotland had its engineering taken over by GEC Tarmac Railway Maintenance (GTRM). They seemed genuinely baffled when they told us to do something that wasn't in our job description, and we simply replied "no". Obviously, the management training courses hadn't prepared them for such a scenario. They attempted to brainwash us by running several roadshows where senior managers and HR consultants would talk absolute bollocks about how we were all the same family now, and then give us plates of sandwiches. Due to their inability to make any inroads with the workers, except with the feeble-minded and desperately ambitious junior managers, the HR consultants usually had a shorter shelf life than the sandwiches, despite their fancy and expensive packaging.

I was making my way through the grades in my job, and was now a senior technician, but my loyalty to the union and outspokenness as a rep, led me not to sign a deal that management had imposed that changed our terms and conditions and pay structure. This stopped me getting promoted. This all changed when the mercurial manager Mister Oates took over the depot. He was an absolute scream, a fantastic engineer, wonderfully gifted, but never a manager in a million years. We would wind him up by printing his name on leaflets and then locking them in the union notice board. He would go absolutely apeshit, and one time,unbeknownst to him, we screwed the door of the notice board shut, and he managed to smash up the entire case by trying to vigorously pull it open. As coincidence would have it, the latest HR manager, Catherine Noah, had just bumped into me on the stairs, and we both witnessed the immediate aftermath of Oates actions. I shook my head in fake solemnity, barely able to keep a straight, and said, "it's very disappointing to see a manager behave like this now we're all part of the same family". Oates looked genuinely ashamed and subsequently apologised to me for destroying the case.

When a technical officer's job came up, Oates said I should apply. I knew this potential promotion would likely be kyboshed by senior management and HR, so I said, "well, there's no point Tim, we all know HR won't allow it". It had the desired effect with him fuming, "I run this depot not HR". I applied and to my utter amazement was given the job. Noah looked devastated and I couldn't help rubbing salt into the wound by saying, "what sort of a company would give me a technical officers job, Catherine, GTRM are a laughingstock". She was gobsmacked but eventually stuttered, "I think you're right Mister Hedley" To be fair, the money was very useful as the Hedley family was growing just as fast as the RMT. I now had five daughters, Carlene, Lorna, Ashlene, Sinead and Stephanie, and solidarity didn't pay the bills.

My newly achieved status didn't last long. During the engineering strike of 1998, which was over pay and conditions, I was staffing a picket at Euston. To break the strike, management had brought in contractors to do our jobs. We had set up a picket line and a van full of contractors drove straight at us, braking at the last minute. The pickets were infuriated at this highly dangerous stunt and some shouted and banged on the van. The van reversed away, and we thought that was the end of the matter. The next day, on returning to the picket line, I was arrested and subsequently charged with criminal damage, as apparently the van's wing mirror had been cracked. This was an absolute stitch up. I was nowhere near the mirror that was allegedly cracked, and even produced photographs taken on the picket the same day, which showed me in completely different clothes to the person who allegedly had done the damage. Nevertheless, management and the British Transport Police seemed to work together to ensure I was sacked, taking the case right up to the eve of the court date before dropping it unceremoniously.

Of course, unlike the court which requires proof, the management needed no such pretence of fairness. They sacked me, which led to an immediate unofficial strike by my workmates, some of whom were there on the day the scabs drove at us, and knew I wasn't to blame. We went from depot to depot convincing workers to down tools and join us. We managed to pull out the Willesden, Stonebridge and Watford depots for a couple of days, before they were intimidated back to work by management and the union disgracefully issuing a letter to all members repudiating the unofficial action. My comrades at Euston stayed out for a couple of weeks, but they were isolated and in danger of being sacked, so I asked them to return to work, as we had absolutely no chance of winning alone, and it would be pointless to add more good people to the list of those dismissed.

When I was sacked, Mark M from the Colin Roach centre was instrumental in helping me gather people around me to help get me reinstated. We decided to semi-formalise ourselves as the strike support group, and they helped in creating, printing, and distributing leaflets explaining my case to other rail workers, who we wanted to come out on strike to get me reinstated. There were some fantastic people, Terry Dunne, an ex-miner, and Anne and Tony Goss, from Arthur Scargill's Socialist Labour Party. Dot Gibson and her comrades were also a great help, and they all gave freely of their time, helping to build demonstrations and even occupy Railtrack offices in an attempt to force the hand of their contractor, GTRM, to give me my job back.

The RMT were in a financial crisis at the time and couldn't even continue to print their monthly paper. Dot got very professional 4-page papers done, complete with photographs. One day we got wind from a very good executive member, Mick Atherton, who had brought me all over his region to gain support, that the GTRM senior union reps led by Mick Cash, were on their way to the union headquarters to lobby against the executive supporting my dispute. We decided to ambush them, and leaflet the whole building exposing their treachery, and how Knapp had repudiated the action of my workmates. We gave out about 100 papers and caused quite a stir. One of the staff innocently asked Knapp if he had started printing the RMT paper again, confusing our handout for the official RMT publication. Knapp was apparently incandescent with rage screaming, "it's not our bloody paper, it belongs to Hedley and bloody rent a mob". It must have been embarrassing for him that a group of activists with virtually no resources could produce a paper, no matter how small, when the entire union with all its resources couldn't.

For reasons best known to himself, Mark M fell out with me after I advised my isolated workmates to stop striking when the cause was clearly lost, to prevent them being sacked. He wrote an article in the Weekly Worker which blamed me for the whole situation, and with wild hyperbole, drew fantastic conclusions that the defeat of one small dispute involving about 150 workers at its zenith, was some kind of massive tragedy for the entire working-class akin to the miner's strike. As they would have said in Derry, "wise up Mark"

I will never forget those brave comrades who defied the union and management to stand by a victimised representative – John, Gary, Sean, Victor, three different Peters, Ian and anyone I can't remember, thanks for your support. To salve their consciences the union leaders gave me basic pay until my appeal was heard, which was obviously unsuccessful and then I was on my own. Once again, the union bureaucrats had shown their true nature. Rather than helping to spread the strike, they effectively killed it off by writing to members repudiating it, and letting them know that if they were sacked, they would have no support from the RMT. Union bureaucrats really are far more effective in destroying disputes than management could ever be, as they are seen to be on the same side as management, they sell the workers short time and again, and show by their actions why Marx described them as "the lieutenants of capitalism".

8   ALL CHANGED, CHANGED UTTERLY

My life had changed drastically. After ten years on the railway, I had been stitched up and sacked for being a militant union rep. My marriage had disintegrated due to my activism and inability or unwillingness to pay enough attention to my family. I'm not making any excuses for my neglect of my loved ones: I accept full responsibility, but I was completely obsessed by trade unionism and the socialist cause to the detriment of everything else. I had what I can only describe as a kind of tunnel vision, and really believed that we could change the world for the better and bring about a socialist society, and prioritised this above all else.

I used my time out of work to finish a Bachelor's degree in politics philosophy and history. The philosophy part of the course was a real eye-opener with one of the first lessons being on Scepticism. This in a nutshell is the questioning of everything. The lecture was based on the works of René Descartes, a seventeenth century philosopher, who tried to disprove the sceptics' arguments by logically deducing that he was a thinking thing and therefore must exist. This misses the point as the sceptics didn't really argue that the mind didn't exist, but rather that physical bodies could not be proved beyond doubt to exist. Imagine for example that you are a brain in a vat, getting fed electrical impulses to trigger different thoughts and emotions. You would believe that you had a body and were experiencing the world through your bodily senses, but this would not be the case. You, the reader, might dismiss this as nonsense, but I challenge you to prove its nonsense. A variation of this idea is used in the "Matrix" films. Descartes attempted to prove that the physical body was indeed real by claiming God would not let us be deceived. This is weak and, in my view, fails miserably to win the argument, leaving the score, according to me anyway, as Sceptics 1 -Descartes 0.

Of course, the vast majority of evidence leads us to conclude that we do have physical bodies and we live our lives accordingly, but this is different from being able to irrefutably prove that this is the case. The ability to question everything no matter how certain it seemed would stay with me for the rest of my life. After my B.A., I went on to gain a Masters in Historical Research. These qualifications would help me secure employment for a while with the builders Union UCATT, but more of that later.

In my personal life, I kept in contact with my children who were really the only constant in my life. I took them out every weekend, on pay days to the seaside, Thorpe Park, or Chessington, and when money was less plentiful somewhere more local. Kids go through phases, sometimes preferring the cinema or ice-skating, and at others trampolining. I couldn't have them overnight at this stage as I didn't have adequate accommodation, and was usually staying in just a double room. My kids all got on fairly well, and there was an obvious influence of the older girls on the younger ones, so when it became uncool for the older children to do something, the others followed suit. I went through a succession of girlfriends before eventually having a relationship with Yvonne, a woman I originally shared a house with as a friend, for about 18 months, only to repeat my previous mistakes and sabotage

the relationship by concentrating on and prioritising political activism. I was by now living in Haringey and became
re-acquainted with a comrade who was in the TGWU union,
Tekin Kartal. Tekin was a member of the Daymer Turkish and
Kurdish community centre in Dalston, and they organised a
delegation to Turkey, which I went on with people from various unions, including Rod Finlayson from the TGWU, who
would become a lifelong friend. Through Tekin, I met Songul,
his cousin anda refugee from Turkey, who was to become the
second real love of my life and mother to my sixth daughter
Dilara. Songul was petite, had a beautiful face with alluring
almond eyes, and was both feisty and loving in equal measure. I think part of the reason that we lasted the ten years that
we did was her initially limited English, which hindered her
from telling me what she really thought of my behaviour.

Around this time, I was heavily involved with a Hackney Trade Union Support Group run out of the Colin Roach
Centre which was formed in the aftermath of the murder of
Colin Roach, a 21-year-old black man, killed from a gunshot
inside Stoke Newington police station. Inconsistencies and
downright lies in the police account of events led to the local communities believing that he was killed by the police.
We were involved in anti-racist and anti-fascist work, and activists were exposing the utterly corrupt and racist Hackney
police. A prominent activist at the centre was Mark M, who
introduced me to another Mark who claimed he was named
Cassidy – much later I discovered that he was in fact, the notorious spy cop Mark Jenner, who having stolen the identity
of a dead child, would go on to form a long-term relationship

with a female anti-racist campaigner "Alison", as a cover for him spying on political activists.

Whilst a member of the Colin Roach Centre, I went on a delegation to Turkey visiting factories and workplaces where the Turkish unions organised. We went to Izmir, which was in the Kurdish region, for Mayday where tens of thousands defied the state ban on the demonstration, and I was honoured to give a short solidarity speech from the RMT. Two plain clothes Turkish policemen approached me after the speech, trying to question me, but I relied on the old Irish adage "whatever you say, say nothing" and wouldn't reply. They were quickly surrounded by comrades from the Turkish unions who remonstrated with them, and they eventually slunk away without bothering me further. I found this trip absolutely inspirational: many workers were communists, socialists or left-wing Kurdish Nationalists, and their courage in selflessly confronting the powerful authoritarian Turkish state was nothing short of awe-inspiring. Leftists in Turkey were routinely arrested, tortured, and even murdered by the police at this time. When they learnt that I was Irish, my hosts introduced me to the very strong local drink Raki, and I introduced them to several Republican ballads. By the end of the week-long stay, they all could sing the chorus to "Back home in Derry".

At the beginning of the peace process (which began on 6 April 1994, when the IRA announced a three-day "temporary cessation of hostilities", and became permanent on 31st August with a "cessation of military operations"), it was decided that the Colin Roach Centre would send a delegation to Belfast and Derry, which would include some of the Daymer

Turkish and Kurdish comrades. Jenner, the spy, was very keen to go, claiming he had Irish ancestry, which, given his fake name Cassidy, was plausible. We attended a music festival in Belfast before going to Derry and took part in a sit-down protest against the yearly 12th July supremacist jamboree. This is when Orangemen from near and far would celebrate the "lifting of the siege of Derry" by parading drunkenly past Nationalist and Republican areas shouting abuse and harassing the locals. This event was hosted by local sectarian bigots, "The apprentice boys of Derry". The sectarian police force, the Royal Ulster Constabulary (The RUC was drawn almost exclusively from unionist and loyalist backgrounds), reacted to our peaceful protest with their usual impartiality, by kicking us and manhandling us off the Derry Walls where we were perched. Cassidy /Jenner even took pictures of his bruises and emailed them to all his contacts no doubt to enhance his credibility as an activist. Cassidy /Jenner stayed at my family's house in Ireland with his girlfriend. Claiming they wanted some privacy, they pitched a tent they had brought in a field next to our house. Looking back this was suspicious behaviour, but I just assumed that they wanted some time alone. Jenner was an absolute scumbag who worked for the special demonstration squad, which was full of scumbags, who all mimicked his tactics to infiltrate completely legitimate trade union and anti-racist organisations. His only saving grace was that he actually battered a few Fascists along the way.

One amusing aspect of the visit to Derry was my mum's reaction to "Alison", a Jewish activist (targeted by spy cop Jenner/Cassidy) who came with us. I had never experienced anti-semitism in Ireland and had never met a Jewish person there. When introduced, I half expected mum to enquire "are you a Catholic Jew or a Protestant Jew, not that it matters of course". Instead, she turned visibly pale made an excuse and went into the kitchen. I was a bit perturbed by this thinking that perhaps she wasn't comfortable with Jewish people, but later learned that she had removed all the sliced ham from the fridge for fear of causing offence. She probably wasn't aware that the Muslims with us were also forbidden to eat pork, as there were no sudden rushes to the kitchen when they had previously been introduced.

BANG GOES THE CEASEFIRE

On 9th February 1996, at about seven in the evening, I was sitting on the toilet in our house in Canning Town East London. My kids were being particularly naughty that day and continued to crash about downstairs despite me calling for them to stop, and even shouting at them. Then, all of a sudden, the bathroom shook, I shouted "Jesus what have youse done now girls", genuinely believing they had smashed something that had caused the tremor. As it turned out the IRA had detonated a lorry bomb in South Quay, near Canary Wharf. This was miles from where we lived, but we felt the shockwaves very powerfully, nonetheless. The bomb tragically killed two people and caused £150 million worth of damage. The IRA had given a 90-minute warning which should have allowed police to have evacuated the area safely. There were also 100 people injured, some seriously.

The bomb brought an end to the ceasefire which had lasted for seventeen months and came an hour after its formal end was announced on RTE television (The state broadcaster of the Irish Republic). The ceasefire began in 1994 to allow peace talks and stalled due to Brit government insisting on the decommissioning of IRA arms before progress could be made. After another lorry bombing a couple of months later in Manchester, the Brits dropped their demand and talks resumed. This eventually led to the Good Friday agreement in April 1998, which ended the Provisional IRA's campaign of armed resistance to the British state's occupation of the Northern six counties of Ireland.

My work with the Colin Roach Centre persisted and one action that we supported was around 1996 when the neo-Nazi group, Combat 18, were used to steward an Orange Order parade in London. Although there was no love lost between anti-fascists and Orangemen, they would never have been targeted if they had not willingly collaborated with an openly neo-Nazi organisation. The 18 in C18 symbolises the letters AH, the initials of Adolf Hitler. AFA stewards gathered to show their disapproval and were forced to defend themselves when the combined Orange /Nazi mob became violent. Needless to say, we anti-fascists were victorious. I stood a few feet away from spy cop, Jenner/Cassidy, as he smashed a Lucozade bottle into the head of a fascist who was trying to attack us. Later we joked that it was retaliation for him getting battered on Derry's walls. I remember feeling absolutely euphoric after defeating the loyalist/fascist axis that day, and thinking how the oppressed almost always side with other oppressed people, and how the oppressors always back other oppressors.

What is the difference between loyalists and fascists? This is a highly debatable point as both ideologies are based on supremacist ideas. Most loyalists would not support Nazis because they were the enemies of Britain in World War Two, but a minority certainly do. Loyalist Ulster Defence Association leader, Johnny Adair, was associated with the same neo-Nazi group, Combat 18, who the Orange order had foolishly asked to steward their parade in London. There are other elements of Loyalism who would not tolerate Nazis, these were exemplified by former Ulster Volunteer Force (U.V.F.) member and Progressive Unionist Party (P.U.P.) leader, David Irvine, who passed away. Irvine and fellow P.U.P leader, Billy Hutchinson, are hard to pigeonhole politically, but would probably fit into the old Labour Democratic socialist mould. They were certainly involved in sectarian crime, but although I disagree with a lot of their political views, I couldn't genuinely categorise them as far-right. Is Loyalism a peculiar British form of Fascism? Certainly, elements of Loyalism would fit that bill, with their blind loyalty to an unelected monarch, their supremacist ideology, their scapegoating, and repression of Catholics, their glorification of an idolised version of the past, but other strains do not share these traits. I would therefore categorise Loyalism as an amalgam of Fascists, sectarian bigots, Protestant supremacists mixed with other working-class elements, who, had they been born in England, would no doubt have been at home in the Labour party, and far to the left of Starmer and Blair. I hope against hope that genuinely socialist and progressive elements eventually win out in the battle for the hearts and minds of the Protestant working class.

9 IT WASN'T COOL TO BE UCATT

Finding it absolutely impossible to find work on the railway anywhere, I later found out that I had been blacklisted by the employers. I was desperate for a job and got steered in the direction of the Union of Construction, Allied Trades and Technicians (UCATT) by an ex-brickie now working for them as a union official, Mick Dooley. Mick was and is a magnificent trade unionist and a walking enigma. He told me when we first met, how during a protest when he occupied a high building crane on a site, how God had come to him and told him that he would lead the building workers. He was simultaneously a staunch Catholic and a revolutionary Marxist, who together with Dave Smith and others had started the Joint Sites Committee, a rank-and-file building workers group who occupied building sites, called wildcat strikes and upon occasion, as I was to find out, literally bricked up employers by building walls around their offices. At a time when building unions were hamstrung by the anti-union laws, with the itinerant workforce changing locations very often, and making compilation of a ballot matrix (a list of employees, their locations and home addresses) almost impossible, the Joint Sites Committee was very effective in what it did. It isn't unusual in the building game for small contractors to go bust, leaving the workers unpaid and the main contractor refusing to pay their wages. By occupying offices or merely having high-profile protests outside sites, many a big company was forced to do the decent thing and pay the workers for the labour that they had already done.

Mick arranged an interview with the UCATT General Secretary, George Brumwell, for the position of development officer. I was told that I would be primarily causing and supporting disputes on sites with anti-union employers, and that I would also recruit members. This sounded fantastic, being paid to do what I loved was like a dream come true. Any illusions that I had were quickly dispelled on the first week when I met the London regional organiser, Jerry Swain, who was to help train me. My training consisted of going to various subcontractor's offices and asking them for membership forms. These it turned out were literally forms that the employers themselves filled out in bulk with their own address on them as a contact. There were no real members, as even if by chance names matched up, these people didn't know that they were in the union. I was dumbfounded, what the hell was going on? Jerry explained that employers gave us membership (meaning membership money) if we left them alone and didn't cause them any trouble. Not wanting to lose the only work I had found in a year I kept cool and when I got the time phoned Dooley who confirmed that this was common practice in the building industry.

For about 10 months, I ignored Jerry's training and went from site to site trying to recruit members properly. I would get maybe 20 people to join on a good week, whereas the rest of the team were bringing back hundreds of employer filled-in fake memberships. I could tell that this job wasn't for me and clashed with Swain repeatedly. At that time the government had brought in legislation making the employers pay 20 days holiday. Our organising strategy was to build membership by alerting workers to this new right and ensuring they were paid what they were due if they joined the union. After some initial success, Swain effectively barred us from going on sites where he had "membership", making a ridiculous argument in an officers' meeting by saying, "Steve you seem to want to walk past sites where we have no members to cause trouble on sites where we already have membership". In other words, don't upset the employers who fund us by demanding that they pay workers the money that they are legally bound to. No, instead go to somewhere we don't have members, create some trouble there, then I'll swoop in, calm it all down, and get some forms from the bosses and Bobs your uncle. I had a massive row with Swain and told him to "fuck off".

The only thing that gave me any motivation were the Joint Sites Committee and the other rank-and-file organisation, the "building workers group" run by blacklisted worker, Brian Higgins, who had a satirical newsletter that came out exposing bosses and corrupt union officials alike. These would always be organising workers to fight back, whether over pay, or safety concerns, as safety was appalling on many sites. The best of these actions came during the annual employer's negotiations on pay with the unions. These took place near Moorgate on a site with a plush office. We rocked up to the site about 10 am with a van full of bricks and cement and started building a wall outside the office door: this was recorded for posterity and propaganda purposes in the film called "Builders Crack" which is still available on YouTube. The site security guards were summoned when we were discovered and the wall was already about three foot high. They were African lads on minimum wage, and they just pissed themselves laughing. The police were eventually called, and we made our escape before they arrived.

A few weeks later, Brumwell, the General Secretary told me that he wanted the company car he had given me to move around placards, megaphone, and leaflets. I really had the pox with the job at this stage and totally forgot what date he had said. Apparently, he was waiting to go to the airport thinking that the car had been returned, suitcases in hand and ended up having to get a cab instead. He phoned me and I answered, and before I realised it, I'd said, "I can't talk now I'm driving". This sent him absolutely ballistic and he sacked me on the spot. I kept the car for another couple of weeks, out of sheer badness, until I got a letter threatening me with the bailiffs, where upon I posted back the keys and let them know where it was – if they wanted it, they could pick it up.

Even the supine UCATT executive couldn't allow me to be sacked without a process, so they reinstated me. This drove the egotistical Brumwell to distraction. In my hearing, I told them all about the false membership racket and negotiated a leaving package which paid me up to the end of the year that I had been contracted for.

A few years later, it was absolutely no surprise when allegations of union officials colluding in the blacklisting of workers were made, and that the Unite Union that had swallowed up UCATT had launched an investigation, albeit kicking and screaming under intense pressure from the rank-and-file.

10 DRINK PROBLEM? I DRINK, NO PROBLEM

It was a friend of mine called Mick who recognised that I was a problem drinker. I had never thought of myself as such, I certainly didn't drink every day or even every weekend. What I did do was binge drink. Perhaps twice a month on average, and sometimes I would get absolutely caned to the point where I could hardly walk. My whole life I had been around people who did not drink socially but drank to get drunk, so I thought that this was quite normal behaviour. When I was drunk, I felt empowered. I could express positive emotions that men were discouraged from expressing where I was brought up. I could easily express negative emotions such as dislike and even hatred quite easily when I was sober, as this was allowed in my culture. To tell someone I loved them was a different thing altogether. This was very peculiar, as I could tell women who I didn't love all sorts of lies but when the emotion was genuine, I was absolutely unable to articulate it either to my wife or even my children when I was sober.

Drinking of course had a downside: it was expensive, unhealthy and an escape from reality for only a short time, and when I sobered up the problems were still as bad, if not worse. I would also get a lot louder under the influence of drink, and sometimes take banter much too far, provoking people. I was never one to shy away from a fight and this led to several altercations over the years and many acquaintances lost in the process. Mick brought me to my first Alcoholic Anonymous meeting where I listened to people's stories about the havoc that alcohol had caused in their lives, and how, through AA, they had regained their sobriety and with that a measure of control and normality. I attended AA meetings on and off for about 2 years from 2002 to 2004, and stayed clear of alcohol with a few minor relapses until 2013, when I relapsed very badly indeed. Alcoholics are masters of self-deception, convincing ourselves, time and again, that we have somehow been cured and can drink socially like normal people. This is a very seductive and dangerous illusion. Once the alcoholic allows drink back into their life, the old pattern of behaviour quickly resumes, and chaos is again allowed to reign. Writing this book, I am two weeks sober and hopefully will stay so. If you have a deity or deities you may want to beseech them on my behalf, it can't do any harm.

11 BACK ON THE CHAIN GANG

Having been sacked from UCATT, and having no money, finding work was a priority. As luck would have it, my old mentor in the Union, Mick Ryan, had set up his own contracting firm "Lion verge", and was now reputedly a millionaire. I rang him up and he agreed to give me a job and renew all the tickets I needed to get back on the railway. In many ways Mick was too nice for his own good, and he also employed some absolute snakes who eventually came into conflict with him, and the company had to close. By that time, I'd moved on into testing new electrical and mechanical equipment that had been installed, but felt outraged by the way they'd used him.

I was contracting for about 18 months when I got a job on the King's Cross Channel tunnel project and something very bizarre happened. I was accused of stealing a piece of equipment called a shunt box, which was no use to man nor beast outside the railway environment. Such a box could be bought for under £200 and I earned that much in four hours, so there was no way I'd jeopardise my work doing such a ridiculous thing. I immediately contacted the old Joint Sites Committee crew, and we began to picket the site. Suddenly management were backtracking and claiming that they hadn't accused me of stealing at all. Simultaneously, a group of iron fixers with Laing O'Rourke builders on the same site were in dispute over pay. I couldn't resist getting involved, persuading them to stop work intermittently to have meetings. As the job started to fall behind, Jerry Swain of UCATT infamy phoned me up and asked if I wanted him to get me a deal. I said, "no thanks Gerry I'm already working nights", which was a complete lie, but I succeeded in giving him the impression that I could keep this shit up indefinitely. Every morning, Mick Dooley would turn up outside the site with a giant inflatable rat, and this together with frequent visits from a samba band who supported us, brought the project the kind of publicity it dreaded. After a couple of weeks, the Laing boys reached a compromise, and I was offered three months' work on another Channel Tunnel project in Kent, presumably to get me away from King's Cross.

After the Kent project finished, railway work dried up for me. This was of course because I was blacklisted (I received compensation for this years later), so I went for a time as a TUC tutor, and did some work with the GMB. I met some good people, but the money was rubbish and I needed to get back to earning a decent living. I updated my CV and bombarded every railway agency I could find looking for work. I got a few weeks here and there, but was running up my credit card and getting into debt, so I was considering a complete change of career.

12 THE SPY WHO GRASSED ME

With Anti-Fascist Action having defeated the BNP on the streets, forcing the latter to withdraw from public demonstrations, AFA itself decided to go down the political route by setting up the Independent Working-Class Association (IWCA). This did however leave virtually unopposed groups like the National Front who were still attacking left-wing activists when they could. A group was formed to remedy this and act as a deterrent to the remaining fascist street operatives. I was involved with this group, called "No Platform", and this is where I met the second spy cop who was part of the Special Demonstration Squad (SDS), and who was using the name Carlo Neri. Carlo was a big lump of a man in his early thirties who often accompanied the stewarding team to protect against fascist attacks. He came across as jovial and friendly, liking a drink and able to cook decent Italian food. He even came on a picket when I was sacked from a job on the railway to pretend to support my campaign for reinstatement.

In 2001, fascists from the National Front attempted to attack the Cock Tavern pub in Sommers town, North London. The pub had a large function room and was used by many trade unions to hold meetings because of its central location and relatively cheap beer. It also attracted many left-wing groups for largely the same reasons. In November 2000, there was a social organised by the 32 Counties Sovereignty Committee, this included speakers from Turkey in the form of left-wing Kurdish activists. The National Front (NF), or more accurately Terry Blackham's rump splinter faction of the NF, announced on their website that they would be marching on the pub, well after the event, to protect the "ancient British right of free speech", by intimidating the landlord who had given the NF's political opponents a venue to air their views. Freedom of speech and ancient rites obviously didn't apply to anyone the NF disagreed with.

About 50 anti-fascists turned out to defend the pub from around 30 Fascists who were protected by a large number of cops. Some fascists managed to elude the police and charged the anti-fascists, of which I and other members of No Platform were part. I remember being hit quite hard in the face, but responding with every boxer's favourite combination a 1-2-3, that is a left jab, right cross, left hook combination putting the fascist on his arse. We soon counter-attacked, charging at the fascists and running them all along Phoenix Road before the police could intervene. In all, seven anti-fascists were arrested, me included. Two fascists were also arrested, but police released them immediately. The police must have thought that Fascists are allowed to punch people, or maybe they were undercover coppers who they initially nicked. The NF website was really hilarious, simultaneously moaning how the police failed to defend them from vicious attack by "reds", while simultaneously claiming a great victory. Like most fascists, they were absolute Walter Mitties the lot of them. The NF then threatened to protest outside the Cock every Tuesday night, providing the cops were there in sufficient numbers to protect their cowardly arses. In fact, they never had the balls to turn up there again.

Like Jenner, Neri has assumed the identity of a dead child, and hooked up with a female activist, Donna, to provide a cover for his activities. Unlike Jenner, I never saw Neri physically confront a fascist – that's not to say that he didn't – but I honestly never saw him do it. Neri also joined the Socialist party to hide his activities and, to deter suspicion, pretended he was a locksmith who travelled a lot. In reality, like Jenner, he went back to see his wife and kids and work provided a smokescreen for this.

What makes Neri even more sinister was his attempt to entrap activists including me into firebombing a charity shop by claiming that it was run by Italian fascists. Neri made this suggestion when we'd been at a party drinking for several hours, and although it was completely out of character for him, I dismissed the incident as him just having gotten too drunk and getting brave because of that. Imagine though if someone had been stupid enough to go along with the idea, property may have been destroyed, completely innocent people may have been injured or even died, and people might have done a lot of time because of a desperate scumbag of a policeman.

I was stupid enough to put Neri up for about 6 weeks, when he claimed to have split up with a girlfriend leaving him homeless. At the time I was working away a lot myself on the railway and had two spare rooms, so it wasn't a big deal for me to put him up. In fairness, he hardly stayed at all in my house, maybe two nights a week, saying that he had another girl he was seeing. Later, I found out that he had told another comrade, Paul, the exact same story, and that whilst supposedly staying at mine, he was also supposedly staying at his flat too. Whilst at my flat Neri made veiled references to the Italian Red Brigades, claiming that he knew some of them and trying to intimate that he was somehow involved. I thought at the time that this was bravado and bullshit, and I was proved right.

Neri, like Jenner, disappeared before his nefarious activities were discovered leaving devastation not only in the lives of the activists that he'd betrayed, but also in the lives of his own family. To add insult to injury, I found out when papers from the blacklisting consulting association were disclosed, that he'd been involved in giving information to employers that helped keep me blacklisted and out of work for a year. Me housing the bastard just goes to show that the old maxim of "no good deed goes unpunished" certainly can be true.

13 BLACKLISTED BY THE BOSSES AND THE SPY COPS

Before the blacklisting of workers was exposed, I, like a lot of people was absolutely baffled by events. I was a highly qualified railway engineer, and later a new works railway tester, a job that was very much in demand, but would go long periods without jobs. Sometimes I would be told by an agency that I would start work in a few days only to be told at the last minute, or even when I turned up at site that the job was now gone. Things came to a head when a ridiculous allegation was made that I had stolen a piece of electrical equipment called a "shunt box", and I got sacked, being eventually given another job after weeks of picketing. It just didn't make much sense. In total, I spent about a year unemployed, victimised for my Trade union activities.

Things became much clearer when, in February 2009, the Consulting Association was raided by investigators from the Information Commissioner's office. The Association was run by Ian Kerr, a 66-year-old man who had made money out of compiling information on Trade Union activists and selling it to employers, who would then stop these activists from getting work.

For a decade and a half, Kerr and his lackeys built up a database that detailed the activities of union industrial and safety representatives who had spoken out against issues on building sites. The list contained thousands of workers. We don't know if there were files relating to other industries as only the construction ones were seized, but as building often went cheek in jowl with railway work, and often the same companies were involved, I would be absolutely astonished if similar blacklisting files did not exist for rail workers.

Managers at Carillion, Balfour Beatty, Skanska, Kier, Costain, McAlpine, (who all incidentally had railway divisions) and more than 38 smaller companies would go through potential employees' names, checking them against the Consulting Association's list, and refuse work to anyone that Kerr had listed as a troublemaker.

The Consulting Association were the people responsible for having me backlisted. They compiled files by receiving information from senior company managers, Human Resource managers, and, bizarrely, by trawling through left-wing papers that covered strikes. I know, because my file contained all these sources. In my particular case, there was also information given to the employers from the Special Demonstration Squad, whose members, Carlo Nero and Mark Cassidy/ Jenner, had spied on me: I assume it was them, unless there is another agent that I am not yet aware of.

Forty-four construction companies subscribed to the Consulting Association. It is documented that officers in the Special Demonstration Squad (SDS) spied on trade unionists for nearly 16 years. In the case of Cassidy, he even joined and chaired meetings of the rank-and-file "building worker group" which was vociferous in its criticism of the UCATT union leadership.

Documents seized by the Information Commissioners Office (ICO) confirmed that in 2008 senior officers from another undercover police unit, the National Extremism Tactical Coordination Unit (NETCU), even gave a Power Point presentation to the Consulting Association meeting (Smith, 2013; Hennessy, 2013). They agreed to exchange information, a quid pro quo that broke the law, because blacklisting is illegal. This was exposed by the Blacklist Support Group who made a formal complaint to Independent Police Complaints Commission. The police were forced to admit that special branch in Britain and the occupied six counties of the North of Ireland provided information to employers as a matter of course (Smith, 2013).

It has also been confirmed that police spied on the family of murdered man, Stephen Lawrence. SDS members deliberately targeted female activists conning them into long-term relationships, and even having babies with them, in order to infiltrate completely legal and legitimate organisations and to gather information. Some of the women targeted and sexually abused appeared on the Consulting Association blacklist, which was solely for constructions workers, although they had never worked in any job even remotely connected to construction.

SDS officers who supplied this information to the bosses, which stopped innocent people getting employment, were a subsection of special branch, and were not just a few rotten apples. Over many years, it emerged that there was a systematic targeting of trade union and political activists, using the excuse of "domestic extremism" to prevent health and safety reps like Dave Smith, who complained about the lack of toilets on building sites, from earning a living.

By collaborating in this scandal, Human Resources management have given the lie, if anyone was stupid enough to believe it to begin with, that HR managers are somehow impartial honest brokers. Things were so rotten that the Chartered Institute of Personnel and Development (CIPD) had to investigate 19 of its own members for blacklisting workers. Some of the worst offenders haven't even been sacked and the appalling Sheila Knight, of Drake and Sculls infamy, identified in Parliament as being responsible for blacklisting workers from the Jubilee line extension, unbelievably now runs her own consultancy, providing "expert" HR training. This includes training master's degree students at the University of Reading. The mind boggles to think that such a person could be considered fit and proper to train others, you really couldn't make this up.

By 2019 the employers had been forced to pay £35 million pounds compensation to over 1,200 backlisted workers. I got £35,000 in compensation. In my opinion, they got away far too lightly. These big businesses colluded with the police to break the law. Their action devastated numerous workers' lives, with houses, jobs, and marriages lost because people couldn't afford to support their families. We will never know the true impact of blacklisting on mental health, or how many were driven to suicide by this barbarity. Why aren't the criminals of the Consulting Association behind bars with the senior managers, HR directors and police officers who colluded in this illegality? It is obviously a case of one law for the rich and another for the poor.

On the 29th of June 2023, a public enquiry led by retired judge, Sir John Mitting, found that at least six undercover officers had sexual relationships with women during their covert deployments between 1968 and 1982. The conclusions would come out in tranches, such was the scale of the spying, and this first tranche finished in 1982. More will come out as they process continues. It went on to state that 139 undercover officers had been used to spy on completely legitimate "left-wing" and campaigning groups including, anti-war, anti-racist and Anti-Apartheid organisations. Mitting concluded that the Special Demonstration Squad (SDS) of which Neri and Cassidy were members, were funded by the Home Office, and known about in very senior levels of government.

Mitting had "come to the firm conclusion" that SDS methods were "not justified", and added that they would have been stopped immediately if they had become public knowledge, whereupon the SDS would have been closed. I was interviewed by the BBC and Andrew Marr of LBC on the day the inquiry reported, together with Dave Smith of the Blacklist Support Group, a member of the MC libel campaign "Alison", who had been duped into a long-term relationship by Cassidy /Jenner, and other people whose lives were devastated by the SDS's unnecessary and unjustifiable spying. I took the opportunity to expose how Neri the undercover cop had tried to entice us to firebomb a charity shop by pretending that it was run by Italian fascists. The report is coming out in tranches and the full story of the police's misdeeds are still not known.

14 GOING UNDERGROUND

One day out of the blue I was contacted by an agency and asked if I wanted to work as a contractor on London Underground. I had never worked for the underground before, but the pay was good, so I agreed and was stationed at Acton Town to complete my training. We would get to Acton for about 10 at night, but couldn't get on track until the last train left. This meant that the union reps could visit us for about an hour to update us with developments about ongoing negotiations, possible disputes and to recruit new members. Paul Jackson was the London Underground branch secretary, and he did a fantastic job, regularly visiting depots right across the length and breadth of the Network. I got talking to him one night as I was still RMT Harlesden engineering branch secretary, largely because nobody else wanted to do it. I agreed to attend the engineering branch where I knew a few faces from union engineering conferences.

The London Underground Engineering department had been disgracefully privatised by New Labour and was now divided into Metronet who employed me and the smaller Tubelines. My new RMT branch LU engineering organised in both Metronet and Tubelines. Metronet was far more militant, and I was soon involved in several days of strike action over pay. The company was in financial difficulties, due to massive mismanagement, after milking the Underground funded by the taxpayer for years. Things came to a head, when during yet another strike in 2007, the company went into administration, costing the taxpayer a reputed 410 million pounds.

We were absolutely cock a hoop at Metronet's demise and demanded to be brought back into London Underground, with
full rights to join the pension scheme and free travel facilities
like all the other LUL staff. The then Mayor of London, Ken
Livingstone, had no choice but to acquiesce to our demands
– it was well known that he was not in support of a privatised
engineering section anyway, and welcomed its return to the
LUL fold. When Tubelines also folded it meant that New labour had wasted the massive sum of 30 billion pounda on
the failed public-private partnership, money that could have
housed every homeless person in Britain and given a massive
boost to the NHS. New Labour sucked.

Rejuvenated by my experience with the engineering
branch, I again began to play an active role in the union, regularly attending branch meetings and then becoming a delegate to the union's London transport regional council. Bob
Crow was now the General Secretary of the union having won
the election in 2002. Bob's campaign involved the promise to
break the draconian anti-union laws, which meant lengthy
balloting and notice periods before any legal action could
take place. Imagine the scenario if a union rep was picked on
for no good reason and sacked. Their workmates could not
respond without breaking the law, for at least six weeks. To
comply with the law, there has to be at least two weeks' notice
of the ballot given to the employer, a two-week balloting period, and, if the ballot is successful, another two weeks' notice
to the employer of action to be taken. By this time the anger over the worker's unfair sacking has probably dissipated.
Added to this, 50% of the workers balloted now have to vote

or the ballot is invalid; so let's say there are 100 workers in a depot, 49 vote for strike action, and nobody votes against, the ballot is deemed a failure as only 49% of people have voted. If this nonsense were applied across the board, there would be very few local councillors for any political party left in office. Nevertheless, under Bob's leadership we began winning more ballots than we lost. We did, however, not break the anti-union laws.

After having attended the region for a while, I witnessed a very debilitating faction fight. The London transport organiser, Bobby Law, had fallen out with Bob Crow, and Law's supporters in the region were at loggerheads with the Crow loyalists. There was an unfortunate altercation in a pub with someone claiming that Law had assaulted him, but others saying that they went outside for a" square go" and Bobby won. I wasn't there so can't definitively say what had happened, but I had known Bobby Law for years and would have been shocked if he had struck someone without provocation. What was very clear was that this incident had split the London transport region apart, and the regional council meetings became like a bear pit. Things came to a head when Law was moved to Dover, hours from his home. Bobby was suffering from extreme back pain at this time and said he couldn't do the journey. He was also forbidden to attend any London transport meetings. Bobby defied the instruction turning up at the region, castigating the general secretary Bob Crow, who had also turned up, and was immediately suspended for his actions.

I was friends with both Law and Crow, so tried to stay out of the whole situation as much as I could. Most of the people

I knew and socialised with in the London Underground Celtic supporters club were backing Crow (I was a lifelong Celtic and West Ham fan). When Law was eventually expelled, a decision I vehemently opposed and pleaded with Crow to reverse, there was a series of resignations at all levels throughout the region. This led to a vacancy for regional secretary, which I was encouraged to stand for, as I was seen as neutral and therefore acceptable to both camps. I was opposed by the SWP member, Unjum Mirza, and unfortunately this campaign got nasty with the Celtic supporter's club being portrayed as a "white man's club", despite having black and Asian members and more than a few women who held membership. I think this was to imply that I was some sort of racist despite my history showing the complete opposite. Anyway, I won the election and became the regional secretary setting about the job with a passion and seeking to heal the divides in the region.

Bobby Law lost his appeal and eventually negotiated a leaving package, before emigrating to Spain for a time and opening up a bar. This left a vacancy for the important position of London Transport regional organiser and when people initially encouraged me to stand, I told them to "fuck off", as I couldn't afford to take the 15 thousand pound pay cut to accept a job which would consume my life and probably put me in an early grave. Anyway, the last thing I ever wanted was to be a union bureaucrat. My supporters kept at me, and then a very weird thing indeed happened: I failed a practical exam at Acton when I couldn't find a fault on a piece of equipment. My brain just froze, and rightly or wrongly, I just stood there smiling thinking that fate had intervened and pushed me towards a union role. I had been finding far more serious faults for over 20 years, on far more complicated equipment, and I took this as fate intervening and nudging me towards the union position – as having failed the test, the drop in money would mean the subsequent salaries between the union and underground roles were roughly equivalent.

I stood for the regional organiser position where I defeated Neil Hodgson who, was, in RMT terms, right-wing, and was to become even more right-wing, joining UKIP, Nigel Farage's anti-immigrant far right party. Some might find this characterisation of UKIP contentious, but I believe that British Fascism will not come dressed in a swastika, but rather in suits wearing Union Jacks on their lapels, pretending to be men and women of the people, and whipping up anti-immigrant sentiment to detract from the failings of the capitalist system, while turning worker against worker, so the elite can benefit. Farage and his cronies completely fit the bill for this in my mind.

Here are some early warning signs for Fascism – judge for yourself if UKIP, the Brexit party, and even the right-wing of the Tory party meets these. 1 Strong use of Nationalism, I would say there's little argument over this one with continuous references to Britain's "Glorious past" (steeped in murder, rapine, theft, and enslavement of other nations). 2 Disdain for human rights, look how they minimise the rights of migrants. Creating the "other" as an enemy to unite against, migrants (singling out Muslims for special attention) are again scapegoated by UKIP and other far right elements. They demand to abolish the human rights protection given by membership of the European Union. 3 Rampant sexism: although claiming to want to protect "our women", there is little doubt about the patriarchal nature of UKIP and the far right, their attitudes to abortion being a case in point. 4 Controlling the media, look at the attacks on the supine establishment controlled BBC, which is portrayed as the "Bolshevik broadcasting corporation" and centre of "woke madness" by the right wing. This is an attempt to stymie any criticism of right-wing ideas by the media. 5 Obsession with national security, demanding measure be taken to keep immigrants and Muslims out as they are in some inexplicable way "dangerous". 6 Fascists support "native" business and suppress labour. The far right policies of Ukip, the Brexit party and the Tories are clear about limiting the right to strike and their promises to support "British business". Fascists disdain intellectuals who don't agree with them. Again this fits the bill with intellectuals being portrayed as an elite out of touch with "the people" and actually enemies of the people, who set out deliberately to fool "the people". 6 Cronyism and corruption with no regard for the rule of law for the "leaders". Look at the scandals that the Covid crisis created with billions of pounds being given to friends and relatives of Tory politicians, and being wasted due to a complete lack of experience, and simply because they provided inadequate personal protective equipment. The behaviour hit crisis point when the Prime Minister and his cronies having made the rules forbidding meetings during Covid on the grounds of social distancing, were caught red handed repeatedly breaking those rules. Fascists continuously call for crimes to be punished with harsher sentences and more jails instead of addressing the causes of crime mainly rooted in inequalities, except when *they've* committed the crimes, as they see themselves as "above the law". I would argue that a number of so-called "legitimate" right-wing British partis could easily fall within the categorisation of Fascists.

Incredibly Mirza, the SWP member, supported Hodgson's (who would later stand as a UKIP councillor) campaign. I won the election taking up my position in 2012, winning 58% of the votes.

15 THE INFLUENTIAL "UNDERGROUND CELTIC SUPPORTERS CLUB"

The Underground Celtic Supporters Club was formed in the summer of 2001 by Celtic fans working on the London Underground. The club from its inception was and has remained anti-fascist, anti-racist, anti-sectarian and pro-republican, having no allegiance to "Queen or Pope". The club meets in the Cock Tavern, 200 metres from the RMT office. All founding members of the club had in one form or other been involved in militant anti-fascism and hated racists and sectarians. Any transport worker could join the club and there were black and Asian members and quite a few women. I have since had a parting of the ways with many in the club when they supported the election of the new RMT assistant General Secretary, John leach, who stood unopposed for my old job, and who, having crossed a sacked worker's picket line was therefore a scab. This incident, in no way reflects on the club's previous good work in raising funds for Irish Republican prisoners, anti-fascist causes and campaigning to keep the Cock Tavern open, when the brewery wanted to turn it into yuppie flats. Members of the club often had to gently educate younger less political Celtic fans who sometimes came out with sectarian statements. We had a number of Protestants in leading positions in the club, and we would educate the youth to the fact that Irish Republicanism was a largely Protestant movement with Wolfe Tone and most of the leading lights in the United Irishmen being non-Catholics. Many people who identify as Republicans or loyalists are not aware of this, and it is one of many hidden facts that might lead to the decline of the disease of sectarianism.

All of the founding members also played a role in their union branches either as activists or reps, some in quite senior full release positions. This fact made some of the loyalists in the London Transport region and some SWP members start to create the most fantastic stories of Republican conspiracies to take over the union. When the club backed my election for London Transport regional organiser, the paranoia hit new levels with people accusing the club members of being "IRA supporting racists" and a "white man's club". I can categorically state that we neither racist, nor all white, nor all males. We started to wind up the opposition by deliberately mentioning the club in all the union meetings we attended, referring to it as the "influential" Underground Celtic Supporters Club to provoke an even greater amount of paranoia in our opponents. Once I had won the election, me and the regional president Vaughan, wore Celtic ties to my first regional council causing the Loyalist /SWP axis of evil to go into overdrive with their accusations. Things eventually died down when the penny finally dropped that we were baiting them.

We had some great times travelling to Scotland and abroad to follow Celtic, and I got into my only fight at football when we got attacked by Chelsea fans at a "friendly" between Celtic and Chelsea at Stamford bridge. I didn't see the point in football violence, which I saw as needless violence between working class supporters, but some members of our club were Celtic casuals and Chelsea's hooligans were the notorious neo-Nazi sympathisers, "the head-hunters", so I had absolutely no hesitation in exercising my right to self-defence when we were attacked. In effect it was just a skirmish, when a fat lump in a leather jacket tried to punch me. It was such a slow punch that he could've probably sent me a nasty email quicker. I dodged it and gave him a left hook in his huge stomach and he was clearly winded. The police then arrived in numbers, battoning my mate, Jim. This incident was then reported by my other mate, Stevie, of TAL (the Celtic Fanzine), as the police beating up "an elderly man", which didn't go down at well with Jim. I've always hated Fascists and one thing I quickly discovered is that they are not very good on the pavement.

The Celtic supporters club continues until this day, and I wish them all the best. I cannot, however, agree with some of its leading members supporting a scab for a union position; perhaps someone took the joke about the club being "influential" a bit too seriously.

16 NEW LABOUR ISN'T WORKING

Having lived through Thatcher's and Major's Tory governments, I voted for Blair's Labour party, not because I had any illusions about him, but simply to get rid of the horrible anti-working class abomination that was the Conservative government. I distrusted Blair from the off, he was too slick, too falsely sincere, and too middle England. In essence, I thought he was a slime bag who couldn't be trusted, but would be a bit less vicious in attacking the working-class and the Trade Unions than the Tories had been. 1997 saw a Labour landslide, and a chance to redress the balance in favour of the workers after nearly two decades of Tories attacking by redistributing power and wealth to those who were already rich and powerful. Any faint hopes that may have lingered were dispelled when Blair not only refused to repeal any anti-union legislation, but actually added more. The disastrous public-private partnerships which effectively guaranteed private companies' massive profits for years appeared not only in London underground engineering, but in the health service and even in education. These were an indictment of the New labour regime. This was not pragmatism, but an attempt to appease Capital and big business by effectively guaranteeing that they would make lots of money for a long period of time. It was and remains very bad value for the taxpayer and a total betrayal of so-called Labour party principles. It is estimated that public bodies could have done the job up to three times cheaper, given the extortionate maintenance contracts that were signed off with the private companies for decades after the original projects finished.

The final straw for many people came when Blair backed an illegal war in Iraq in 2003, based on absolute lies that Saddam Hussein possessed weapons of mass destruction that he could use against Britain within an hour. The Chilcot report into this fiasco concluded that Blair had suppressed intelligence reports that did not fit his narrative, and started a war that killed hundreds of thousands of innocent people, on what he knew was a lie. I personally joined the Respect party. Respect was founded by Salma Yaqoob and George Monbiot in 2004. It really came from the Stop the (Iraqi) War coalition and consisted of the Socialist Workers Party (SWP), the Muslim Association of Britain (MAB), and many smaller groups and individuals. George Galloway was elected Respect MP for Bethnal Green and progress was made elsewhere in local elections. Galloway had destroyed the United States senate in a rip-roaring speech, which exposed America's history of invading other nations and the absolute hypocrisy of its government. Internal differences and splits destroyed Respect's potential, with George Galloway's dreadful appearance on the Big Brother TV show seriously undermining his and Respect's credibility. Bob Crow shared the view that we needed political representation outside Labour, having effectively ensured our expulsion in 2004 by backing Scottish Socialist Party candidates. Bob was not a fan of Respect as he mistrusted Trotskyists intensely.

Crow, who had previously been a member of Arthur Scargill's Socialist Labour Party, helped found the "No to EU Yes to Democracy" group, a leftist opposition to the European Union in 2009, and subsequently the Trade Union and Socialist Coalition (TUSC) in 2010. Neither organisation managed to make any impact electorally. I actually stood for election to my local council under the TUSC banner three times, but with a lack of resources and no serious campaign, was no threat to the incumbent Labour party candidates. We will never know how Bob would have reacted to the Jeremy Corbyn phenoxenium, because he was taken from us far too soon, but I would bet my house that he would have no time for Starmer and his Red Tory lash-up, that now hold sway in the party, and are persecuting anyone on the Left who defend Palestinians who are suffering terrible oppression. The Starmer backed witch-hunt has even suspended the former leader Corbyn for telling the truth about widely exaggerated and weaponised claims of antisemitism in the party.

17 TAKING ON THE EDL

In 2009, small Islamist groups in Luton, which had a large Muslim population, were protesting against the war in Iraq by haranguing returning British Troops. This provoked football hooligans to form the English Defence League. From its inception, the EDL was a very mixed bag: most football hooligans, although right-wing and supportive of British imperialism were not ideological Fascists. However, there were Fascists in their ranks. Portraying themselves as a necessary response to "Muslim extremism", the EDL concentrated on marches and protests outside Mosques. Unlike the BNP, who were by now in terminal decline, and the National Front, the EDL did not seek to scapegoat the Jews for problems caused by capitalism and imperialism, even having an EDL Jewish division, but instead attacked Muslims for causing every conceivable social ill.

Me and many RMT members went on counter demonstrations as we saw the EDL as a proto-fascist organisation, who were physically attacking political opponents. The EDL showed their true colours as right-wing extremists when they targeted Unite against Fascism members and other left-wing paper sellers, launching thuggish attacks on them. They disrupted a Trade Union meeting that I attended in Barking but were beaten off by our group of stewards. In December 2010, the mask really slipped when EDL leader, Tommy Robinson, a former BNP member, (real name Stephen Yaxley Lennon) threatened action against students protesting against the imposition of tuition fees and the withdrawal of education maintenance allowance. I'd actually met "Robinson" many years earlier outside the Coffee House pub in Camden opposite the RMT head office. I didn't have a clue who he was then, as he was not yet notorious. He was with a relative who worked for the union, and who introduced him as Stephen. I remember saying "that's easy for us to remember, two Steves". I then bought a round, with him included – I'm sure the only part of this that my enemies will report is that I went drinking with "Tommy Robinson".

In 2011, the EDL attacked anti-capitalist protesters in London. As riots erupted in rection to the police murder of Mark Duggan, EDL members mobilised in largely white areas in Enfield and Eltham, clashing with black youths and even the police. An organisation that sides with the state to attack the left and ethnic minorities is a fascist-led organisation, even if all its members are not conscious of that fact. Robinson was a willing puppet for his super-rich capitalist backers who funded his divisive hate-filled campaigns and would do anything to secure his money supply.

The EDL began to weaken in 2011 when infighting broke out between different football firms resulting in "the Infidels" breaking away under, John "Snowy" Shaw, who claimed Robinson and his right-hand man Carol had their fingers in the till. Shaw's supporters clashed with Robinson's in Blackburn in a vicious battle. Robinson attacked another EDL member at the rally and got convicted of assault. Robinson also tried to enter America illegally using a false ID. He was caught, convicted, and sentenced to 10 months in jail.

In September 2013, the far-right bigots tried to march to the East London Mosque in Whitechapel, and we brought a large RMT delegation that joined thousands of counter protesters blocking their route. Earlier, as the London RMT Transport regional organiser, I had gone from station to station warning members who had been abused and even assaulted previously by the EDL that they had the right to close the stations. Many of our members were Muslims and were clear targets for the extremists. I am delighted to say that our members closed several stations including King's Cross and Liverpool Street on health and safety grounds. This seriously disrupted the EDL plans to get to the beginning of their planned march. I was honoured to speak at the counter demonstration and brought solidarity from our General Secretary and members to the gathering made up of thousands of local people, trade unionists and socialists. After several clashes, in which they tried to attack us but were forced to retreat behind police lines, the EDL were forced to go home, tails between their legs. Robinson, ridiculously dressed as a Rabbi, breached his bail conditions and got nicked again. In 2013, Robinson left the EDL but continues to obtain money by grifting and associating with far-right organisations, Zionists, and anyone else who will give him funding.

I'm very proud that RMT members had a role in the demise of the EDL, opposing them not just ideologically, but physically, on the streets, preventing them from taking control of who could and who couldn't organise in areas. Once they'd tasted a few defeats, the infighting soon started, and the corruption was exposed. Robinson was not finished yet, however. His narcissistic need for publicity and easy money would lead him to keep popping up, causing trouble, and getting well to do so.

18 THE FINANCIAL CRISIS

In 2007/2008, the world's financial system was thrown into great peril and almost collapsed entirely. Brokers had gambled trillions of dollars on the subprime mortgage racket in the United States and lost badly. Banks and financial institutions had underwritten risky mortgages and then sold the risk in the form of derivatives, making billions of dollars in the process.

Lehman Brothers, which had been founded in 1847, was the 4th biggest finance broker in the world with over 25,000 employees all over the globe. In 2008, it had to file for bankruptcy. The repercussions of such a company going under triggered a crisis and the whole subprime mortgage bubble well and truly burst.

British Labour Prime Minister Gordon Brown, who had succeeded Tony Blair, rushed to the aid of the speculators putting in place a huge taxpayer-funded bailout for the financial institutions. The consequences of handing over trillions of pounds to bankers who had crashed the economies worldwide was described by Edward Luce as "Socialism for the rich, capitalism for the poor", as workers who had no part in causing the crisis were forced to pay for it with wages frozen and public services cut.

Mervyn King, Governor of the Bank of England, introduced a policy of quantitative easing, which was basically printing more money and distributing it throughout the financial markets to help prop the system up. Instead of stimulating the economy as King had intended, it just made the mega-rich even richer by inflating property, share and asset prices. This shocking giveaway of trillions of pounds to the wealthy was literally being paid for by workers as we were told to "tighten our belt", and, ridiculously, "we're all in this together".

There was, however, resistance from workers and left-wing groups. Rail workers refused to

pay for the bosses' crisis as did many others. One of my proudest moments as a regional organiser, right in the teeth of the financial crisis, was to play a leading role alongside other RMT members activists and reps. I met giants of the movement, such as, Glenroy Watson, Clara Osagiede , Joy Jowcham and Joseph Mamboliya in the campaign for a London living wage for tube cleaners. Most of our activists were immigrant workers, many fleeing oppressions from dictatorial regimes, and their bravery, in taking on not only the bosses, but also the government was breath-taking. In 2008, there was a succession of 24- and 48-hour stoppages of work right across the Underground with the cleaners employed by contractor ISS and the other large contractor Initial, coordinating action to successfully force the bosses to pay the 'London living wage' of £7.20 an hour. The migrant reps, with help from the region, drew up a detail organising plan, visiting every depot to recruit hundreds of cleaners in order to fight for fair pay and dignity at work. Sometimes management would refuse us permission to go on site which would mean standing outside the depots for hours, catching the workers before and after the shifts and convincing them to join the union.

This was not just about recruiting, it was about organising and getting a network of reps into place that could take on the bosses when we weren't there. This led to us initiating a policy where every depot elected a rep or preferably two, and the reps decided what action to take in the cleaning grades committee. This committee was made up exclusively of cleaners, and theythen provided feedback back to the region. Before they organised so effectively things were terrible,the cleaner's vulnerability and migrant status was often exploited mercilessly by the employers, with short pay, bullying and sexual harassment being rife. It made my heart soar to see people stand together, not just to win the pay rises, but to demand that the bosses recognised their humanity. Going on strike and joining the union was a step in ending the treatment of African, Indian, and East European workers on the tube as second class citizens. People who take action, especially if that action is successful, often change out of all recognition, self-confidence replacing hesitancy, and standing together rather than allowing themselves to be played off against each. This leads to immense personal growth and an understanding of the capitalist system no textbook can rival.

Just like everywhere else, the bosses and government sought to cut back on public services to pay for the crises caused by the bankers. In 2010, we were forced to ballot the whole RMT Underground membership in order defend 800 safety critical jobs. This time we were joined by the smaller TSSA union. Four one-day strikes followed, but because ASLEF who organised about 60% of drivers on the Underground refused to ballot and instructed their members to cross picket lines, many services ran. To their credit, many Individual ASSLEF members did not cross picket lines, but joined the action. There was eventually a compromise reached, where all the redundancies were either done by not filling vacancies when people left the job, or through voluntary severance. Eventually some of the drivers who were not directly affected by the job cuts began to drift back to work. ASLEF reps played a poisonous role in this, seeking to poach RMT driver members, telling them they were being used as "cannon fodder" for the station staff. The whole point of being in an industrial union like the RMT is that when one grade is attacked then everyone comes to their aid, rather than allowing people to be picked off one at a time. Sadly, ASLEF did gain over a hundred members by their shocking anti-working-class tactics. This was hugely disappointing to me as the organiser, but it's difficult to stop people in their late fifties or early sixties, who are due a decent pension and have had enough of the job from leaving with a few quid in their pocket. Of course, this cutting of staff left more work for those who stayed on the job, more unsociable hours, more weekends to work, and a big detriment to their work life balance, with quality time spent with loved ones severely diminished.

In June 2009, we were offered a pay deal for all London Underground workers of 0 percent as inflation, because of the financial crash, was actually negative, and RPI plus 0.25 percent for the next two years. We immediately began to ballot on this ridiculous offer and were successful. This forced the employers back to the table where they came up with an offer of 1.5% for 2019, RPI plus 0.5% for 2010 and RPI plus 0.5% for 2011.Considering that most the rest of the country was having their pay frozen, this was a good deal. It amounted to

1.5 % above inflation in year 1, and a guaranteed above inflation deal for years 2 and 3. For example, if inflation reached 8%, we were guaranteed 8.5% and if it reached 10%, we would get 10.5% and so on. This was a deal that infuriated the right-wing and their puppets in the press, who claimed that we had held the country to ransom. What it really showed was, that given the right leadership, and armed with the correct information about the causes of the financial crisis, workers will take action even in the teeth of massive criticism from the government and the press, who accused workers of being greedy for demanding a pay rise, whilst simultaneously handing the bankers billions.

In 2011, we were able to successfully rally the troops to defend victimised sacked activists, Eamonn Lynch and Arwen Thomas. Eamonn was reinstated after a successful ballot and Ardyn's employment tribunal, brought forward to avoid a series of rolling strikes amongst train drivers. He did have to spend a year working 9-5 in lost property on full driver's wages with no weekends, early or night shifts to bother him.

Another consequence of austerity was that It infuriated many ordinary people, who were not usually at all political, to see the rich, who had caused the crisis, benefit and the rest of us have to pay for their folly. The anti-Capitalist movement Occupy began in the United States, where activists occupied Wall Street to demand social justice. The movement spread to many countries and an Occupy camp was set up around the Bank of England in the St Paul's area of the City of London.

I went to the London Occupy site and was completely underwhelmed by what I discovered. The RMT delegation of which I was a part were tasked with going and trying to make links with the protesters. The idea was to build a united front against austerity, bringing radical workers to support the Occupy protesters and seeking to learn from their methods, and perhaps even building a coordinated fightback. We arrived at about 9.30 am and the place seemed to be deserted. We walked around and all the tents were still there, but nobody appeared to be present. We thought for a moment that they'd abandoned their protest, moving on to somewhere else. We walked about chatting amongst ourselves until eventually a couple of the unwashed emerged from their tents to complain that we were waking them up. This didn't go down well with the RMT people who had to work shifts and get up very early on a regular basis. Occupy it seemed was just another incarnation of the middle-class left made up of students, liberals, lifestyle anarchists and do-gooders. Their radicalism seemed to be a sham to mask "lifestyle" hedonistic protest. They were incapable of understanding, let alone, working with working-class trade unionists, dismissing us as unrevolutionary because we went to work and didn't join in their occupation. Similarly, after meeting this rabble, who seemed to want to lay in bed all day, many RMT members dismissed them as wasters who were not good potential allies, and no real joint work actually took place, although some of them did turn up to support pickets.

Austerity was to last for a decade, the Brown government giving way to a Conservative /Liberal Democrat coalition appropriately named the "Condemns" by their detractors. The official TUC response was again pathetic, organising a couple of marches and rallies against austerity, giving well-paid union bureaucrats the chance to spout nonsense but do nothing, making no effort whatsoever to build for a general strike, which was the only hope of defeating the massive attack on the working class.

19 FINALLY, AT LEAST AN APOLOGY, IN PART AT LEAST, FOR THE BLOODY SUNDAY MASSACRE 38 YEARS AFTER THE EVENT

I sat glued to my television, hardly believing my eyes and ears, I had just watched a British Prime minister, and a Tory at that, apologise for the British army massacre of civilians in my hometown of Derry in January 1972. I never thought that I would live to see this day. I was genuinely taken aback by the candid way the British Prime Minister spoke, and thought that at last justice would be done. I was of course to be disappointed but none the less this was a start.

On the 15th June 2010, the British Prime Minister, David Cameron, head of the "Condem" Tory/ Liberal Democrat coalition, announced the results of the Lord Saville inquiry into the events in Derry in 1972. Saville uncovered a web of deceit and cover-up weaved by the British army and their government masters. It exposed the false testimonies of British soldiers who took part in the massacre or witnessed it, and who had lied through their teeth trying to justify murdering 14 unarmed civilians by claiming that the people they shot were armed IRA volunteers. Cameron told Parliament that, "What happened on Bloody Sunday was both unjustified and unjustifiable. It was wrong".

Outside the Guildhall in Derry, relatives of the dead and injured and their supporters cheered as they watched on screens that had been erected for the decision.

Saville admitted that the army had killed 13 marchers outright, and wounded another 15, one of whom subsequently died later in hospital, all of whom should not have been shot.

The Saville report which took 12 years to finish and cost nearly £200 million pounds concluded unambiguously that the British army was absolutely and completely unjustified in firing on unarmed people, stating:

"None of the firing by the parachute regiment was aimed at people posing a threat or causing death or serious injury."

Cameron concluded that, "The government is ultimately responsible for the conduct of the armed forces, and for that, on behalf of the government and on behalf of the country, I am deeply sorry"

At the time this was ground-breaking, flying in the face of the Widgery whitewash that the Brits had conducted immediately after Bloody Sunday, which was a complete farce.

The Saville report had made it very clear that none of those killed or injured by British soldiers was armed with guns, and that the army had given no warning before opening fire. Importantly though, the report did not put the blame on the British government of 1972, claiming that there was "no evidence" that the government "encouraged the use of lethal force". This effectively let those politicians who oversaw the army's overall policy and strategy off the hook.

Incredibly, Saville also found Major General Robert Ford, the army's overall commander to be blameless. Ford, who had been in Derry, when the massacre occurred had even taken the decision to send in the Paras responsible for most of the shootings.

Saville instead concentrated on the instruments, the people who pulled the triggers rather than those pulling their strings. These included soldier "F" who invented stories about being confronted by a nail bomber to justify his killing of at least 4 civilians, and possibly as many as 6. Only one senior officer, Lieutenant Colonel Derek Wilford, who ignored instructions is criticised for ignoring his superiors' orders and sending in the Paras. Saville found that there had bee "a serious and widespread loss of fire discipline among the soldiers".

Although most of the relatives of the deceased and injured, and indeed those who had themselves survived the massacre, welcomed the Saville's reports findings, many were left unsatisfied, seeing it as an attempt to fix the blame at the lowest possible level and exonerate the politicians and army top brass. To this day, the Bloody Sunday commemoration march continues to take place annually in Derry, which I attend regularly, seeking justice for those murdered and injured on Bloody Sunday, and the prosecution of not only the soldiers who carried out the atrocity, but their commanding officers and the politicians who enabled them.

What I would say to British people and, in particular, anyone who protests against any aspect of government policy is this: if they can shoot what they consider "British subjects" in the North of Ireland and get away with it, then they can do the same in England, Scotland and Wales. We can already see the crackdown on the rights to strike and protest being brought into force by the government in the Public Order Act and the Minimum Services Act. The Public Order Act forbids protest which the government decides is disruptive, allowing the police to arrest and criminalise not just peaceful climate protesters, but anyone they judge to be disruptive. It also widens stop-and-search powers, and allows people who have committed no offence to be banned from attending demonstrations. The Minimum Services Act seeks to force workers in what the government deem as "essential services" to break their own picket lines and effectively scab on colleagues and their own disputes. Make no mistake, these measures are an attack on civil liberties, and severely diminish the right to protest effectively against anything that the government chooses.

Civil liberties have been paid for in blood by our foremothers and forefathers, who were massacred, beaten, imprisoned, and deported in places from Peterloo to Merthyr, from Glasgow to the Bogside and from Yorkshire to Tolpuddle. These liberties cannot be meekly surrendered on the whim of a government. I see no prospect of individual trade union leaders or the TUC taking the necessary action to protect our rights, and our only salvation will come in the form of grassroots union members refusing to undermine our own disputes by breaking the law and refusing to cross picket lines. Such action will no doubt, when it occurs, not only produce threats from the government but also the trade union bureaucrats, who will see it as a threat to their privileged lifestyles, paid for by members' money, which may be sequestrated if the law is broken.

As I had predicted, the job of London Transport regional organiser was taking over my life.

I was running from meeting to meeting, trying to cover an impossible workload and at the same time organise the branches that constituted the region. I again fell into old patterns of neglecting my family and prioritising work. This led to me and Songul, my partner, parting ways, even though we had a very young daughter Dilara. Again, I accept that this was totally my fault and if I sit back and try to analyse the reasons why I repeated past mistakes, I can only say it was a combination of me being driven to do something that in my mind, anyway, was absolutely essential, and perhaps my ego getting out of control, by believing if I only worked harder, then Socialism would be achieved. As the old Irish saying goes "the cemetery is full of indispensable people", and undoubtedly, I fell into the trap of overestimating my own role in the struggle to the detriment of my family and ultimately myself. I again went through a series of girlfriends, who were prepared to put up with coming second to my work, until inevitably they eventually complained, and I dropped them and repeated the whole process.

I was doing 12-hour days at least six days a week, taking phone calls, texts, and emails from union members at all hours of the night and day. I think even my enemies and detractors acknowledged that I put in a shift, and this helped the region move on from the divisions caused when Bobby Law was sacked. Because we were organised and extremely militant, we in London Transport were winning above-inflation pay deals, even during the period of the financial crash when very few people in the country could say the same. People may have found me abrasive and far too left-wing for their tastes, but they liked the pay rises and conditions I helped them secure through hard work, sheer stubbornness, and the ability to organise and motivate credible resistance. This included protests, occupations of buildings, some political lobbying and of course strike action.

There where however setbacks, TFL and London Underground were forced to practically merge and hundreds of jobs were lost. Most of them were managerial jobs, and trying to get workers to defend people who had scabbed on previous disputes was very difficult. We won the ballot for action and had a few days strikes, but many weren't convinced. Unbeknown to me, Pat Sikorski, the Assistant General Secretary, was sent to ACAS, the conciliation service, to negotiate, and in my opinion came back with an appalling deal that saved only a few jobs, and was nothing more than a fig leaf that gave us an exit strategy for the dispute. Pat had been a friend, a real firebrand when I first knew him, but to my mind, at the time, was now just a bureaucrat who justified his actions with left-wing language. I fell out badly with him and stood against him for the position of Assistant General Secretary. I thought I could do a better job, but with hindsight, I acknowledge that I was also driven by ambition and ego, not only for myself, but ambition for the class. I also honestly felt I could provide more effective leadership and get better results. I won the election and as Pat was near retirement age anyway, he finished up with a redundancy payoff for his service. I often ponder if I could go back in time would I change my decision to stand, as I felt sorry for Pat, who had in his time been a fantastic rep and activist. Like it or not, I always come up with the same conclusion that I would've stood anyway. I know how this makes me look, but that's the truth of it, perhaps we all have a certain time in the movement, me included, where we do our best work, before the inevitable processes of the bureaucracy take their toll, and demands for "moderation" affect our ability to deliver the best outcomes for workers.

Just before I left the London Transport job, there was another flare up on the engineering department over management trying to impose changes in working conditions that would inevitably lead to job cuts. We were sitting in ACAS with management trying to hammer out a deal that would prevent us striking over the weekend and costing the company millions, due to having to cancel costly line blockages and equipment. I was seething at having lost the previous dispute and my mood was not improved when Gerry Duffy, the main protagonist in the previous negotiations who had done the deal with Sikorski appeared. Duffy was a big hard-drinking Glaswegian and larger than life. I actually quite liked him outside of business hours, but he had helped to do me over. When he arrived, we were literally dictating the terms of managements' surrender, but there was something in his demeanour that rankled me. When management had typed out the proposed agreement, it contained everything we had demanded but as I was reading it, I looked at Duffy and thought that he was smirking. I couldn't help myself, I screwed up the paper and threw it at him. To the bewilderment of our team, I took US out of negotiations and informed the General Secretary that the strike was going ahead. The next week when negotiations resumed, Duffy was there with his tail between his legs, sitting glumly as Phil Hufton did management's side of the negotiations, and we signed off virtually the exact same agreement with Hufton (who was then a director), with a few caveats just to make it look better, that I'd thrown at Duffy previously.

While work was nonstop, I was determined to still see my kids at weekends, at least, and thought that I had managed to balance this. Recently though, in conversations I've had with my daughters, they remember me always being on the phone, either talking to reps, managers or members, and often being distracted. What I thought was quality family time was not really seen as such by my children, who since I left employment with the RMT say I'm much more "in the room" when we're together.

21 ACCUSED OF BEING AN ANTISEMITE BEFORE SUCH ABUSE BECAME FASHIONABLE

After decades of opposing the far-right, and even being arrested in the process, I was to fall foul of the antics of a load of Zionists, who turned up and disrupted an RMT regional council meeting held on the subject of Palestine. I attended the meeting in my role as London Transport regional organiser and it was entitled, "Palestine and possible benefits of boycott, divestment and sanctions". The meeting's expert speakers, many of them Jewish, told us about Israel's treatment of the Palestinians and Israel's continuing breach of international law, including countless United Nations resolutions. I came to the meeting as the regional organiser to welcome people, and because it was part of my duties. I was not even sure what BDS meant, or of the merits of the proposed policy. It soon became apparent however, that around five people in the room had come to disrupt the meeting and to prevent meaningful debate.

They began by interrupting and shouting comments, such as "liars!" and "that's a lie", increasingly noisily barracking speakers, who included Israeli anti-Zionist Jews, Ilan Pappe and Moche Machover. The hecklers then whipped themselves into a frenzy, even abusing people (including RMT members and activists) in the audience by calling them "Nazis", "Fascists" and "racists". In contrast, the meeting itself was conducted in order to let everyone, even the disrupters, speak ad nauseum, without heckling or interrupting them in any way. The barrage of abuse reached a crescendo when I tried to answer some of their points. I was abused as a "Nazi" and a "Fascist" by someone now known to me as Richard Millet. I found this very upsetting, as I had a long history of anti-fascist activity dating back some quarter of a century. I have had to vigorously defend myself from Fascist attacks on numerous occasions and have even been arrested for my activitism. It was made known to me during the meeting that at least two of the disrupters were associates of the neo-fascist English Defence League (EDL) who had a "Jewish division". RMT members and others had been opposed to the EDL, who targeted Muslims and socialist activists for abuse and even physical attack. It was these disrupters, who were clearly acting as agent provocateurs to disrupt a trade union meeting that I was addressing, when I was recorded by Richard Millet one of the disrupters on his mobile phone, a recording which he then posted on the internet on a number of right-wing websites. This information came from Carol Foster, one of our retired members and a Jewish campaigner for justice for the Palestinians. Carol herself was abused as a "Fascist" during the meeting by the hecklers, and on a previous occasion has been threatened with violence by the same group.

Millet's video recording itself has been heavily edited to 17 seconds in length and does not show the context in which my remarks were made, remarks which were recorded in full at the meeting, and which I kept a copy of. The full recording shows that I had to raise my voice to prevent myself being shouted down by the hecklers and disrupters. In hindsight, it was obvious that they wanted to provoke just such a reaction, and then to use it against anyone who criticised the policies of the state of Israel.

After these events, I read in a Workers' Liberty blog that I had made two allegedly antisemitic comments. This was very strange as absolutely no Workers' Liberty members were at the meeting, which in itself was shocking, as they had many activists in the RMT London Transport region, and were very much opposed to the Boycott and Divestment strategy. I would have expected them to all have turned out at the meeting to argue their point of view, which was their democratic right. The fact that they didn't show up made them conspicuous by their absence, and the fact that they seemed to parrot unchallenged the account given to them by rabid Zionists, who attempted to wreck the meeting, indicates to me where their allegiances truly lie.

The first remark that they considered antisemitic was "your friends in the media". This was clearly not an antisemitic remark in the context it was used. It was obviously a reference to those reporters who cover up the actions of the Israeli government, and I made it very clear that all my criticism was about the Israeli state's policies. It is widely known that British and American media report on the Israeli occupation of Palestine in a biased manner, favouring the Israeli state and American interests in the region. This is illustrated by the fact that the release of one Israeli soldier became a cause celebre in contrast to the release of hundreds of Palestinians, including many teenage children who were simply described as Hamas terrorists. The second comment I made was to Richard Millet after he had just called me "a Nazi" for the second time.

He then asked me, "Do you feel better now?" I replied sarcastically, "Yes, better than you anyway, but maybe you feel better than me, as you're one of the chosen people". He replied, "Is that because I'm a Jew?". I answered, "No, it's because you're a Zionist. I have no idea what your religion is". Again, this was in no way antisemitic.

The phrase "chosen people" refers to the Jewish people, comes from The Torah and is repeated in The Bible (Deuteronomy 14:2). It has been adopted by right-wing Zionists as a Biblical justification for the seizure of Palestinian land, which they see as their God-given right. However, I accept that my use of the phrase in the context of the highly inflammatory argument, with aggressive and disruptive intruders trying to wreck a public meeting and provoke a reaction, was unwise and I regret using the phrase and allowing my enemies the opportunity to twist my words to their own ends. I apologised to anyone who may have misconstrued the remark and been offended.

I have never been, nor will I ever be, anti-Jewish, or racist against any nationality or ethnicity. Neither will I refrain from criticising Israeli state policy towards the Palestinian population where that policy is discriminatory, oppressive, and racist. I regret that I was provoked into making statements that could be deliberately and maliciously misconstrued by right-wing Zionists, who are openly hostile to trade unions, openly consort with the neo-fascist EDL, and who wished to smear my reputation and that of my union. Richard Millet, for example, had to register his blog out of the UK because he has been sued for slander and libel by other victims of his maniacal denunciation of everyone who dares to speak out against the Israeli state's role in the Middle East.

Looking back at it, I think the Zionist tactics set to disrupt our meeting were refined by Zionists and the right-wing of the Labour Party to try and silence anyone who condemned the Apartheid Israeli state, or who even dared to raise the issue of the brutal and murderous repression of the Palestinian people. Unfortunately, their tactics have been very effective with decent Labour Party members now absolutely terrified to condemn the racist Israeli state, its illegal occupation of Palestinian land, its terrorising of the entire Palestinian population and killing with impunity of Palestinians and journalists who report on these atrocities.

We now have a Labour Party, whose leader is a self-confessed Zionist, suspending not only party members who support the Palestinians and condemn the Israeli state's barbarity towards them, but also withdrawing the party whip from previous leader, Jeremy Corbyn. When Corbyn was cleared of charges of antisemitism, he was still not reinstated and his film "the big lie ", which exposes the dirty tricks against him and other left-wingers, is being banned from being shown on premises controlled by the Labour Party and certain trade union bureaucrats, including members of UNITE.

22 UNLUCKY FOR SOME 2013

2013 was a bad year for me, and the events that I will briefly touch on were extremely traumatic, and I have debated
whether to write about them at all, and perhaps dredge up old
wounds and cause needless pain. I decided I would have to
as they would affect me terribly and had a knock-on effect in
the RMT for years to come. I did not behave well during this
time, and I am genuinely sorry for my shortcomings. I hope
the woman involved has moved on with her life, and is now
happy and fulfilled. A year earlier, I had met a woman in her
thirties, I was 43 at the time. We got together and she moved
into my house very quickly, as she was getting evicted from
her flat. She was completely up front about suffering from a
mental health condition, Border-line Personality disorder,
but I had no real idea what this entailed. The relationship
became very difficult, with her self-harming regularly, sometimes cutting herself badly, which necessitated me taking her
to the hospital. I was not blameless, as once again I put my
work before my personal life, and was sometimes very un-
sympathetic to an illness that I didn't really understand. One
morning in 2012, I got up early, still half-asleep, to find her
painting my hallway. I couldn't quite believe it, I had bought
that paint for the bedroom, not the hall. I asked her to stop,
but she wouldn't. After a few minutes arguing, in total exas-
peration, when she still refused to stop painting, I kicked the
paint tray (ironically as it turned out, as I didn't want to try
and physically prevent her painting by snatching the brush),
expecting it to go in a straight line away from me. Instead,

my kick caught the rim sending it into the air and splattering the hall and her back in paint. I was shocked, horrified and started to apologise. She reacted by smearing my face with a brush full of paint and the confrontation became physical. I was wrestling to restrain her. By this stage she had her back to me. We slipped on the paint; she landed face first on the floor and I landed on the floor on top of her. After a few seconds I got up and she got up and ran into the bedroom. Much later that day, she emerged with bruises on her face. I was shocked and ashamed; I shouldn't have physically stopped her, despite the provocation, but should have instead walked out of the flat. In the evening we made up, and as there were never any previous incidents like this and never any other similar incidents in the next six months or so that we were together, I thought that it was the end of the matter. When we split up, I got together with another woman and thought that I was in love, so got engaged to be married very quickly. When my previous girlfriend found out about this, she went to the police and accused me of hitting her a year earlier.

People I had known for decades started to avoid me; many people who I didn't even know and didn't know me accused me of being a wife-beater. I was bombarded by people who I'd never met on social media accusing me of all sorts of things that even my ex-girlfriend had not alleged that I'd done. Complaints were made to the RMT trying to get me suspended. I didn't handle this well and challenged some of the men who were making the accusations to come and say it to my face, which of course is the last thing I should have done as their reaction was, "there you see, we told you". Eventually, the RMT investigation, conducted by my nemesis, Mick Cash, found I "had no case to answer", and the police didn't press charges as there was "no evidence". This did not placate my enemies inside or outside the union, who would weaponize the issue against me for years to come, dredging it up at every opportunity, and especially when I was taking part in an election. The whole episode is a very sorry affair and I wish it had not happened, and that I had been a better person, able to walk away from conflict and be more understanding of a person with a serious illness. The whole thing became too much for me, and after a decade of sobriety, I began drinking heavily again.

One positive from 2013, was the beginnings of me becoming aware of the environmental destruction that was taking place. This would transpire by accident as I was attending a branch meeting in Sussex, and was invited to attend an anti-fracking demonstration in Balcombe. Cuadrilla, a drilling company, had been issued a licence to look for shale gas. There wwas evidence of such drilling poisoning water supplies elsewhere, and even causing earthquakes. This struck me as a completely insane thing to do. Local residents were incandescent with rage and protest groups began to become involved. In July, a picket of the site blocked lorries carrying drilling equipment and a number of protesters were arrested. The pockets continued with the "Frack off" group continuing direct action against the company. In August, drilling was suspended.

About 1,000 people joined the "No Dash for Gas" camp and small groups broke away, invading the drilling site and gluing themselves to the entrance. Caroline Lucas, the Green

MP, was arrested for a peaceful sit-down protest. All this activity alerted the general public to the dangers of fracking. Plans to frack at Balcombe were abandoned shortly afterwards. Like most people, I was vaguely aware of global warming and the dangers that this posed to human existence on the planet. The opposition to fracking brought home to me just how big business and government were prepared to gamble with our lives to make a quick profit. From that point on, I would always support and on some level campaign for environmental protection issues in the union, including the Green new deal which sought massive investment in public transport and green jobs, and the replacement of fossil fuel with renewable energy sources.

23 A "FRIENDLY" AT CLAPTON

Clapton fans styling themselves as anti-fascists had gone out of their way to make links with established anti-fascist football supporters like those at Glasgow Celtic. It had been arranged that some Celtic fans from Glasgow and Fife would meet up with some London Celts, and attend a Clapton game, originally with the intention to help boost their gate. They had actually been invited by some of the so-called Clapton Ultras. This all changed when the Ultras heard that I would be attending.

On Saturday 28th March 2015, me and Celtic supporters, mostly from the Cowdenbeath flying column and other London-based fans went to see the allegedly anti-fascist club, Clapton. I had been warned, through third parties, not to go there by the so-called Clapton Ultras, who despite not knowing me, or probably the woman who said I hit her in 2012, and despite me being cleared by two separate investigations, decided that they were judge, jury and executioners. They were in fact a group of middle-class wankers, composed mainly of university students and ex-students, who had roped in a few Polish punks and a couple of black youths. They were living out their own little identity politics fantasy at Clapton; they wouldn't have been tolerated at West Ham or even Leyton Orient which had working-class fan bases. On the day, we walked straight into the "Scaffold" stand where the Ultras usually congregated. The Ultras abandoned their stand and went to another area without any confrontation whatsoever, their threats seemed to be all hot air. They then got a group of women to come back and throw beer cans at us, spitting not only at us, but at the stewards who tried to intervene. This was such an obvious attempt at provocation that it was completely ignored by us. They obviously wanted someone to lose their cool, after being spat at and having been hit with beer cans, so they could film them completely out of context and label them aggressive. We were not falling for that.

At the end of the match, fortified by lots of alcohol, and I suppose whatever else they could get their hands on, the Ultras finally came out from behind their women and came over to confront us, throwing full cans of beer indiscriminately into the stand where we were. They then attempted to charge us, whereupon the Cowdenbeath lads, having remained absolutely disciplined up until that point, were forced to defend themselves and battered the Ultras all over the pitch. I, for once, didn't defend myself, as I knew they would want to get me on camera and then totally twist the story. As it happened, we had our own people filming events, and the absolute shower of lies that the Ultras put out was quickly discredited on social media. The Ultras also disgraced themselves even more, having started the trouble and then having gotten battered, they went running to the cops getting a Celtic lad charged with assault. Having played at being football casuals, most of the Ultras have now all moved on to well-paid careers, as the middle-class left have always done, and no longer darken Clapton's terraces with their presence. A big shout out to Paul MC P, Derek, Gash and all the column for their efforts that day. Irish and Scottish people go where we want and won't have our movements dictated by middle-class English lefties playing at being anti-fascists.

To end the day off, a few of the Ultra supporters came into a pub in Stratford looking for me. They found me – and I was with some of the Cowdenbeath lads, whereupon most of them shit themselves, not getting the odds they had obviously expected. One squared up to me, getting physically aggressive, and came away with a busted nose. So ended this episode, and like a true Ultra, his face was "red and white", just like Clapton.

24 THE WORKING-CLASS LOSES ITS LEADER. THE KING IS DEAD

One of my pledges during my election campaign for the Assistant General secretary position in 2012, was that I would not accept the increase in salary, but would give it instead to the Union's strike fund to help support our members in struggle. For the nine years that I held the job, I had the money deducted at source and put into the Union dispute fund. There were a few reasons for this, firstly and most importantly, I don't think any Union official should earn a wage way above that of the average member they represent. Secondly, if you get paid too much, you will inevitably move more towards a middle-class lifestyle and consciousness, regardless of what socialist rhetoric that you spout. Finally, in the back of my mind, based on all my previous experiences of unions, I always knew that at some stage I would be forced to either compromise my principles or walk away from the job. I was at least self-aware enough to acknowledge that being very highly-paid would make walking away a lot harder.

Working for and with Bob Crow was an absolute pleasure. He was no saint but an absolute socialist to the core, and even if we disagreed on tactics, I always knew he had the best interests of the workers at heart. In my six years of RMT service, before Bob's tragic passing, he only ever asked me to do things differently twice. He asked, he didn't order, leaving the decision to me. On both occasions, although I had some misgivings, I did what he asked. The genius of the man was that he could get the best out of everyone, even a naturally obstinate and rebellious bastard like me, by treating them with dignity and respect, and we did what he asked because he made us love him. If anyone is considering a leadership role in a Union, or in fact, anywhere else, there is a massive lesson right there, if you care to understand it.

My new role was a national one, as I was responsible for all the train operating companies in the country, London Underground and all the contractors who subbed work from these. I led on these issues in the boardroom giving my opinion and guidance, but the role was open for interpretation, and I was on the front line at mass meetings and supporting pickets at every opportunity. The class struggle was taking place on the railway, as the Tory government of Cameron were determined to get rid of the role of the guard, which was vital in ensuring trains ran safely, with guards shepherding passengers to safety during derailments, terrorist attacks and other incidents. Disabled people and the elderly were also frequently relying on the guard to ensure that they could safely access the trains at all. Our strategy to defend this vital role was twofold: firstly, we had to prepare our own members for the prolonged action that was going to be necessary to defend their jobs and the public's safety. This was done by creating discussion amongst the guards themselves and finding examples of where they had helped passengers, prevented crime, and deterred potential sexual crime by carrying out their role. In other words, we made guards aware of their own worth. Then we discussed what it would take to win, not just to protest, but to win, and it was by and large acknowledged that sustained and hard-hitting industrial action was the only chance of victory.

Secondly, there was the battle for public opinion. We contacted passenger, pensioner and disabled groups explaining the government's plans and the inevitable consequences. They immediately offered their support with Disabled People Against Cuts (DPAC) coming on many pickets and taking direct action by occupying buildings and stopping traffic to highlight the cause. Politicians were also lobbied with petitioning and emails from constituents, demanding that the guard's role was maintained.

The bosses' first attack came on Southern Railways, where management told us they were determined to get rid of the guard's role and thinking that any resistance would last a few days at most. We immediately organised mass meetings of staff and then public meetings to ensure we won the ballot for strike action that the unions executive had initiated. We went to every depot and workplace making sure everyone voted yes. It was at one of these meetings at Three bridges Railway club on Sunday 10th March 2014 that I last saw Bob Crow, who, as usual gave an inspirational speech rallying the troops, although he did seem somewhat under the weather. Bob left a bit early, which was against range, as he usually stayed for a pint with the members after a meeting.

The next day as I got up for work, I turned on breakfast TV to find out that Bob had died from a massive heart attack. I literally sat on the bed for an hour weeping uncontrollably. I was physically and mentally unable to leave the bedroom. Eventually, I managed to get ready and make my way to the office, where Cash and his supporters seemed to be already manoeuvring him into position to take charge, and his main rival, Alan Pottage, and his supporters were moving to ensure the opposite. The whole building was in shock, as was, I believe, the entire trade union movement such was the charisma and leadership that Bob had exerted. The press was gathered like vultures outside the union office door, the paid harlots who derided Bob and everything he fought for at every opportunity, even hounding him on family holidays, now feigned sympatry for the fallen hero of the working-class. Rail workers everywhere put up posters at their stations of Bob with the simple message "loved by the workers, feared by the bosses", inscribed on it. Politicians who loathed the ground he walked on cried pretend crocodile tears for Bob in a grotesque pantomime of hypocrisy. I don't know how I got through that day.

As the days went past, the furore died down and business slowly resumed. The right wing of the union was rallying to Cash, trying to bury the fact that he'd tried to unseat Crow as Assistant General Secretary, and instead portray him as Crow's loyal righthand man. Pottage supporters including the President Pinkney (who was a rude bundle of aggression at the best of times), meanwhile tried to limit Cash's influence by putting him forward as the person in charge. Stunned by what had just happened, I was vaguely aware of these machinations, but couldn't find the strength to get involved in it all. This changed when Pinkney confronted me aggressively in the corridor because I gave the press a few brief words about Bob passing away when exiting the office. I said something like "the whole working-class has lost its leader and we're all devastated" then walked on, but even this was enough to feed paranoia in rival camps. Pinkney started ranting at me saying, "I told you no-one was allowed to talk to the press". I responded to Pinkney by telling him, "Fuck off you're not in charge". Technically, the Senior Assistant General Secretary, who was Cash, had the right to step in according to the union rules, which Cash got the national executive to okay, by pretending he wasn't running for the top job. Having been installed, Cash wasted no time in getting his name on every leaflet circular text and email that he could, so that everyone would recognise his name when the ballot for General Secretary went out.

In the end there were 5 different candidates: Cash, Pottage, Alex Gordon (who couldn't possibly win, but was too narcissistic to possibly recognise the fact), John leach (who was another complete outsider, who hadn't even settled into his new role of London Transport Regional Organiser), who I believe would have crumpled within six months under the pressure had he won, and me. I stood as I couldn't support either of the main candidates, Cash was far too right-wing, and Pottage, despite being very talented in some areas was also divisive and in my view not capable of doing the job. I knew in my heart that I couldn't win, but was determined to put a fighting socialist militant programme to our entire membership, pushing the agenda to the left, and hopefully making it difficult for whoever won to abandon Bob's legacy.

25 TIME TO CASH IN

Cash won resoundingly and immediately went about disempowering Pottage, who up until that point had been in charge of education and the organising unit. The organising unit had done great work rebuilding the union after the employers ceased the direct debit mandate and we lost 30,000 members overnight, causing a financial crisis in the union. Organising was Crow's initiative, but Pottage ran the unit well with the help of Geoff Revell who had returned from retirement in India. Pottage had built his popularity with hard work and a bit of patronage, arranging for reps to be released from work, to recruit and build the union.

Alan was stripped of his educational responsibilities by Cash, and was told to report to me instead. Cash obviously wanted us at each other's throats, but neither of us was that stupid. We actually became quite friendly, and this increased Cash's paranoia, which was fed by the right-wing in order to ingratiate themselves, by carrying false stories to him and maintain their easy life.

The industrial issues hadn't gone away, and we were now fighting on many fronts. Scotrail, Southwestern Railway, Mersey rail, Northern Rail, West Midlands trains and Greater Anglia all joined Southern in trying to abolish guards. This was a period of intense activity. I personally, along with many officers, was travelling all over Britain to attend pickets and meetings. People were being galvanised by our very effective campaign. The public were generally on side, and the resilience of our members, some taking over 30 days of action, was both humbling and exhilarating. The government had badly miscalculated the willingness of the guards to sacrifice money for the greater good – this wasn't about pay and conditions, it was about safety, accessibility and safeguarding decent necessary jobs for further generations of workers. Sometimes being a union official is shit, but when working-class men and women stand together against all the odds, there really is no better job in the world. I salute those heroes here, as I have many times in meetings all over Britain, they are an inspiration to our class both in Britain and internationally. Their resistance meant that there are still staff on every train that went into dispute, albeit with safety roles diluted in some places. This could not have been achieved without organisation, strategy and the indomitable fighting spirit of people who would just not be beaten.

Of course, every story has its downside. Southern ASLEF, who had initially gone on strike to support the guards, took a deal that would see them line their pockets at the expense of the guard's safety responsibilities. By taking control of the opening and closing of train doors, ASLEF made it easier in future for the bosses to beat strikes and have another go at removing the on-board supervisors (the new name for the former guard's grade). The fact that they went to negotiations with management, and with no RMT union representative present to hammer out a deal is an absolute disgrace. The fact that the RMT General Secretary, Cash, allowed this to happen is an even bigger disgrace. We should have been occupying the venue and bringing along the media to prevent such a rotten sell out. Then again, maybe Cash saw an exit strategy where someone else would get the blame, and used it to his advantage, playing the victim and getting misplaced sympathy. It is very telling that when I called out the betrayal and a "scabs charter" in a TV interview, saying all those responsible should resign, Cash tried to get the national executive to discipline me. If he wasn't involved in the sell-out, then why the wild reaction?

A similar scenario evolved on Southwestern, where again ASLEF did a deal that gave them a financial bung to undermine the guards. In Mersey rail, a tremendously strong position where every driver backed the action, was thrown away by lousy tactics on our part that allowed the company to bring in guards on temporary contracts, until these insecure workers made up the majority of staff. The architect of this disaster considers himself a great negotiator, if so, then it's certainly not for the union or its members.

All in all, considering the balance of forces, the RMT members did a wonderful job in the teeth of overwhelming hostility from the government and the employers. They didn't win everything nor beat off all the government's attacks, but they did force massive concessions that have protected the safety of the travelling public and forced the government to abandon, all be it temporarily, their wish to impose driver-only operation throughout Britain.

26 OH JEREMY CORBYN/OH NO JEREMY CORBYN

I swore I'd never join the Labour Party, and equally never thought I'd see the day I would campaign for the RMT to re-affiliate to that party, but to be fair I hadn't considered a parallel universe where Jeremy Corbyn would be leader of the Labour Party and John Mc Donnell would be Shadow Chancellor. That, however, is exactly what happened.

In 2015 Ed Miliband resigned as he had an appalling election defeat. Four candidates were successfully nominated to stand in the election for leader, they were Burnham, Cooper, Kendall, and by the skin of his teeth, Corbyn. Votes were taken from Labour members and registered supporters, of which I was one. Despite interventions from war criminal, Tony Blair, and the man who wrecked the economy, Gordon Brown, trying to attack him, Corbyn was elected in the first round of balloting with 59.5% of the votes. The right-wing had another go at destabilising Corbyn a year later, entering a three-legged donkey from Wales into the race, who was so non-descript, I only remember he was called Owen something, and Corbyn predictably trounced him.

In the 2017 general election despite dire predictions of an electoral wipe-out for Labour and actively being sabotaged by their own right-wing and party apparatchiks, who wanted to see Corbyn humiliated and forced to resign, Labour actually won 30 more seats than under Miliband, finishing only 800,000 votes behind the Conservatives nationally.

Corbyn and McDonnell had been prominent in the RMT parliamentary group and actively sought re-affiliation from the union. I saw them as working-class fighters with proven records on supporting Irish self-determination, trade union struggles, anti-racist and anti-fascist causes, and who supported refugees and human rights even in the face of abuse from the right-wing inside and outside their own party. I must admit I fell for this call to re-affiliate hook, line, and sinker, reasoning that we could help defend Jeremy and the left in general from inside the party, and stop another coup attempt from the right. I even spoke on platforms for re-affiliation, like a gullible fool, believing that with union help we could secure Corbyn's position and even achieve a socialist-led government. This would start the push back of over 30 years of neo-liberal policies, which had seen wealth and power increasingly drain away from the poor into the hands of the wealthy elite. It should have been obvious to me that the ruling class would do everything in their power to prevent such a scenario and that Jeremy and John, despite being very nice and decent men, did not have the balls required to stand up to them and fight back as viciously as was needed to stop them.

Unable to beat Jeremy democratically, the right-wing attacked a lifelong socialist and anti-racist, who had campaigned against all kinds of racism, including antisemitism, labelling him an antisemite. The correct response to this would have been to go on the offensive and expose all the racist comments by his political opponents. Boris Johnson had abused Muslim women as "pillar boxes" and "bank robbers" and there was hardly a peep of objection came from the mainstream press. Muslim semites were obviously fair game in the racist British media. Instead, Corbyn looked like a rabbit frozen in the headlights. One by one his supporters were picked off, and instead of defending his allies, he let them be fed one by one to the wolves, which only increased the hunger and confidence of the wolf pack until they came for him and withdrew the Labour whip. McDonnell meanwhile stands around muttering under his breath, but not prepared to openly take on the right wing. What a terrible exposing for the so-called hard man of the left, who theatrically waved around Mao's little red book in the Commons, like some kid who'd just joined the student union Marxist society. Reflecting on this debacle, it's probably better that this charade was exposed before they got into power, because the inevitable collapse and capitulation to bodies with massive power like the IMF, World bank, NATO and the EU, would have been torturous to witness, and would have discredited the idea that socialists could make a difference for a generation.

Having come so close in 2017, Labour MPs, including McDonnell and Abbott, allied with the right wing, successfully campaigned to change the Labour Party position from one of respecting the Brexit referendum, to one of having a second referendum. In effect this was saying to the electorate, "sorry you're a bit thick: go back and see if you can get the right answer next time". Not only was this mind-boggling arrogance from the Londonistas, it also effectively sealed the fate of good socialists like Derek Skinner and many more, as people in the red wall seats who had literally voted Labour for generations switched to the Tories in 2019, so that Labour lost 60 seats. Funnily enough, I'd met McDonnell at the BBC a few weeks before the election. I had just finished an interview and he was arriving to do one. This was shortly after he'd addressed the Remain rally in Westminster and promised another referendum. I tore into him saying that he had just lost the election, and he seemed genuinely puzzled to be on the receiving end of my angry tirade. What an absolute joke! Unfortunately, my words proved all too prophetic as the results rolled in and seat after seat was lost. The electoral debacle led to Corbyn's resignation and opened the door to the poor man's Tony Blair, a man completely devoid of charisma and ideas, Sir Keir Starmer, who has rowed back on every decent policy in Labour's manifesto, and persecuted anyone on the Left who condemns the appalling Israeli war crimes in Palestine.

I'll be honest – I voted to leave the European Union for the following reasons: The EU is a superstate that is demanding all railways are open to private companies to run. In effect a Corbyn government couldn't re-nationalise the railway and stay in the EU. This overriding of national sovereignty by the unelected European Commission is a sinister development, and I cannot accept it. Secondly, fortress Europe was already moving to the right and forbidding migrant ships from landing on European soil, instead of putting refugees into holding camps. The rise of the far right concerned me greatly. Thirdly, the imperialist trading bloc that was the EU could only prosper by exerting its influence over trading blocs or individual nations in the developing world, and in particular the global south, to its own benefit. The EU was designed to be a capitalist internal free market with institutionalised free movement of labour, goods and capital; to try and transform it into a socialist organisation was like feeding a tiger an apple, hoping that it would turn vegan. Nevertheless, if the vote had been to remain and I was in an influential position, I wouldn't have been arrogant enough to pull the electorate's nose and demand a re-ballot until I got my way.

Thankfully, the RMT membership were more clued up than me and declined to re-affiliate to Labour despite my persuasion. This is incredibly important, as RMT members would now be funding the very right-wing Starmer-led New Labour mark two, and filling the pockets of the red Tories.

Trying to draw the correct conclusions from this whole car crash is difficult. Most of us will take the easy option if its available to us. It would be wonderful to think that we could just vote our way to a just, socialist society, and in a perfect world this should be able to happen. We do not live in a perfect world; we live in a capitalist society where the drive for profit is literally on the verge of destroying the planet through global warming. We live in a world with limited resources, yet capitalism demands continuous growth to survive, these things are simply incompatible. Already we have the highest temperatures on record in 2023, and soon large land masses will be flooded or too hot to live in, forcing around a billion people to migrate or perish. There is little debate in the scientific community except as to the pace at which this scenario will unfold. Even the paid flunkies and quacks of the oil and petrol industries now concede that climate change is being driven by fossil fuels and the meat industry, yet governments do nothing.

Capitalism is killing us, but the 0.1 % of society that are the mega wealthy, will fight to the death to defend their privileges and don't give a dam about the rest of us. They will destroy anyone like Corbyn who dares to question their privilege and dares to even think of redistributing wealth and power to the masses and out of the elite's hands. If we want real change and indeed a planet for our children and grandchildren to live in, we must massively redistribute the world's wealth, invest in green energy and phase out fossil fuels as quickly as renewable alternatives are available. We must also drastically cut down on our meat consumption (I am a total hypocrite in this regard, as I eat meat). This is not a matter of individual choice, but must be led by governments to have any real effect. Only a planned global economy can achieve this, and such a society can only be brought about by a revolution. Corbyn is not our messiah, nobody can fulfil this role, we need to look to ourselves collectively for the answers. In effect, we are our own saviours because nobody else will do it for us.

Jeremy Corbyn is a nice and very principled man, who has been on the right side of history in the vast majority of the campaigns he's supported. He is not, and never was, going to be someone capable of standing up to the forces of capitalism. The hyperbole around Corbyn was our fault not his. We were desperate for change, and we hijacked him as our vehicle to achieve it, an attempted shortcut that would inevitably lead nowhere. We mustn't make the same mistake again. Good luck Jeremy, I wish you all the very best and know you will continue to inspire with your words and actions, and may yet play a part on the long march to socialism. That march must be made up of the working-class reliant on our own power and not in awe of international financial institutions, our own government, or labour leaders.

27 SUDDENLY I WAS A SENIOR AND IN THE MIDDLE OF A FAMILY FEUD

The way the RMT rulebook works is that there are two Assistant General Secretaries. The Senior Assistant General Secretary is simply the one who was elected first. When Cash got the top Job, I became the new senior. As part of this role, I had to sit on the union's trustee board and keep an eye on the union finances and investments. Yes, I know, a revolutionary socialist, knee-deep in the mechanics of capitalism, the irony of this wasn't lost on me either, any accusations of hypocrite are absolutely justified.

There was a kind of a honeymoon period when Cash took over, and he was not without his talents. Although we were miles apart politically, in his own way, he was able to dig out the best deal for members which didn't involve having to take any action. We had worked together quite cordially when he was the Senior AGS and I was the junior, often covering for each other if unavoidable meetings clashed with boardroom duties. For a while, I thought I could influence him towards taking up a more militant industrial stance, and I have to say the industrial circumstances with it all kicking off with the guards, meant that he was forced to put on just as many and probably even more disputes than Crow. I must explain at this point that the national executive of the union put on strikes and call them off. The General Secretary sits on the executive and can speak on any subject, but unlike the other executive members he or she cannot vote. In a sense then, you could say that the General Secretary is not responsible at all for strikes being called, but this would ignore the reality. The General Secretary places reports before the executive and has tremendous influence over them, it is rare indeed when the executive ignores the wishes of "the boss".

In 2015, Sean Hoyle was elected as national president of the RMT. I didn't like Hoyle who I considered slippery and untrustworthy, a view formed from working with him when he'd previously been on the national executive for three years, just before he ran for president. He was full of ambition which in my opinion was totally out of proportion to his abilities. Hoyle and Cash had history, with a strong mutual dislike being obvious to anyone who saw them together, which would sometimes burst into vicious arguments, especially when Hoyle had two beers or more. Hoyle's strategy was to win over the executive by continuously telling them that they were the real power in the union, not the General Secretary. Of course, this view was actually correct according to the union rulebook, but Hoyle's motives, I thought were not solely democratic. He made it clear almost immediately that he was going to stand against Cash for the top job when the position came up again. This naked ambition quickly split the executive into rival camps with the majority supporting Hoyle, a small minority supporting Cash, and a couple of snakes who went with whoever was in the room at the time. This whole setup made the boardroom a poisonous place to work. I would do the business for the train operating companies, London Underground and my other companies there at least twice a week, usually Tuesdays and Thursdays, with other meetings called when and where they were needed, and it was an absolutely horrible environment.

Hoyle had campaigned on a ticket of a "members-led union". Very simply, this meant that whatever the members wanted, the union should give them. To me this completely ignored the principles of an elected leadership. What was the point of electing officials who would just conduct straw polls of the membership and go with the majority? Surely a dialogue with the members was necessary where the leadership explained what they thought was the best strategy in any situation, the membership discussed this, questioned it, debated with the leadership, and then we collectively and democratically decided on a way forward. To just leave everything in the hands of members who often were not in the possession of the full facts, and moreover, were inexperienced in industrial disputes, was an absolute abnegation of responsibilities by the officers. In my opinion, this was simply a "clean hands" strategy for the leaders if things went wrong, who after all, were being paid to lead and not to avoid responsibility.

Sometimes the antics displayed in this undeclared civil war were amusing, with Hoyle trying to get on any platform anywhere to boost his profile for his inevitable go at becoming General Secretary, and Cash instructing his minions to block him at every turn. This would often result in Hoyle being invited to meetings to speak, and then some feeble excuse being made by the organisers as to why he couldn't at the last minute, leaving him standing like a spare prick cursing Cash to anyone who could be bothered to listen.

Hoyle's supporters coalesced around an organisation called Campaign for a Democratic Union. This was made up of the Socialist Party, Socialist Workers Party, the appalling

Alliance for Workers' Liberty (who were Zionists and wanted to decriminalise digital child porn, I kid you not). It attracted careerists who at the very most had a labourite understanding of politics and wanted to get positions in the union. Once they had been elected, these people showed no consistency in the boardroom, voting their mates' proposals through without question, whilst trying to crucify their opponents if they tried to put through very similar deals. Hoyle successfully manipulated the largely apolitical careerists on the executive with promises of patronage "when he became General Secretary", when in reality there was more hope of Celtic and West Ham meeting in the Champions League final and drawing 6-6.

The effect of this behaviour meant that Cash was to become increasingly paranoid, a paranoia fed by the right-wing careerists who never missed an opportunity to lick his arse, and who wanted to ingratiate themselves to protect their own union careers. By absolute coincidence, I met Hoyle in Turkey where I had booked a holiday, and later discovered he had a villa a few miles away. We met up and he asked me if we could get a picture outside a Shell petrol station to support our offshore workers who were in dispute, I said yes, and he turned up with a poster in the form of a Shell sign with a middle finger "flipping the bird" and "we won't accept no scabs" inscribed on it, (pedants relax I know that the grammar is shit with a double negative making a positive and all that, but that's what it said). The next day, the picture was all over the Turkish and English press. I'm convinced Hoyle had this "leaked" to boost his profile. Cash of course was beside himself with rage, taking Hoyle's pending challenge far more seriously than was necessary.

When I got back to London, Cash attempted to bollock me over the incident. He was always desperate to maintain the veneer of respectability, a trait common in trade union bureaucrats, which of course makes it far easier for the ruling class to control and manipulate them into acting meekly, uncontroversially and ultimately against the interests of those they're supposed to represent. I told Cash to "catch himself on" as Hoyle was nothing to worry about. Hoyle would often try to get me onside with his campaign. Sometimes I would pretend to play along just to see what elaborate and inconsequential schemes he was hatching, but for the most part I couldn't be arsed to humour him.

A combination of the stressful environment where I was working, caused by the erratic behaviour of Cash and the poisonous relations in the boardroom, overwork, constant travelling and a subsequently bad diet, and most importantly, my having gone back on the alcohol, led me to having a heart attack in September 2016. I had to have a month off work and was relieved that no challenger came forward to contest my position as I don't know if I could have travelled all over Britain and Ireland to campaign whilst still quite fragile. I was dually re-elected unopposed in 2017.

The heart attack was a real wake-up call. It's surprising the clarity that can ensue when you're lying in a hospital bed. Although I was visited by lots of friends and comrades, I really appreciated my family's support and how they rallied around me in my hour of need. I vowed then and there to prioritise them more and I believe that I have, for most of the time anyway, put aside more quality time for my children and grandchildren.

28 THE PHONEY WAR GETS REAL

In 2018 the Campaign (for a) Fighting (and) Democratic Union, CFDU, proved that it was not totally useless helping to get Darren Proctor elected as National Secretary (responsible for seafarers and offshore workers and all things Maritime). Darren was a decent activist and socialist, and a dynamic and capable organiser, who had worked for the International Transport Federation (ITF) previously. Darren unseated Cash loyalist and long-time incumbent Steve Todd. This changing of the guard was unforeseen and sent shockwaves through the union. I liked Darren, but was also friendly with Steve, who himself was an old-school, working-class socialist, but the democratic process was abided by and that was that. I also thought Darren's sheer dynamism and work ethic would pay dividends. The reaction was a bringing about of an alliance of Labour Left, Communist Party, and complete Cash flunkies in an attempt to secure Cash's position and to stop "the Trots" as they described the CFDU. Whatever you may think of Trotsky, he was the leader of the Red Army and a senior Bolshevik, and would have been turning in his grave to be associated with a gang of largely apolitical careerists. The "Trot" taunt couldn't have been more misplaced.

At around the same time the Trump media circus descended upon London. On the 14th July 2018, I had attended a rally outside Parliament to protest against Donald Trump's visit to Britain. The far-right was out in force, with Trump supporters mingling with football hooligans, many of them in the Democratic Football Lads Alliances (DFLA), various other far-right groups, conspiracy theorists and assorted lunatics, who were all on the streets to support Trump. Tommy Robinson, former leader of the fascist EDL, had helped organise their rally. The day had passed off peacefully, and when the demo was finished, the RMT contingent, of which I was a part went to a nearby pub, the Westminster Arms for a drink.

The weather was sweltering, and we settled down with some larger tops in the beer garden at the front of the pub. We'd been there for about half an hour when suddenly we were showered with glass bottles and empty glasses. I was hit on the head and in the face, where I would later need 6 stiches. A mob of about 30-40 fascists appeared, having had no trouble getting past the police who were parked 20 yards away, and viciously attacked us. Our delegation was mainly made up of people ranging from forty years old to pensioners, about 10 men and half a dozen women. I was approaching my 49th birthday, and given our demographics, we were obviously considered soft targets. Having thrown their missiles, the mob charged forward. To help protect my partner, Bridget, I instinctively ran towards them, and managed to knock a few of them down before they reached the tables. Some of them had picked up chairs to attack us, and being genuinely in fear of my life and that of my partner's and friend's, and to defend our group, I responded in kind, using chairs, tables, glasses and a banner pole to fend them off. I saw many of our people including two of the pensioners bravely battle with much younger men, so the others could get to safety. The battled raged for a couple of minutes and as sirens wailed, the mob began to disperse leaving several of their number lying on the ground unable to run away. I looked around and I was the only one in our group still in the beer garden, as, thankfully, most had got into the safety of the pub. There were a few fascists still at the entrance and I persuaded them to leave with the help of a large wooden banner pole. I thought it was all over, and began to relax when one of the fascists returned and threw a glass at me. I stepped back to avoid it and stumbled over a chair that had ended up on the floor. Before I could get after him, he escaped to avoid the police who were just arriving. It was only at this stage that I realised that I was bleeding from the head and face, and went to the toilet to clean myself up.

After returning from the toilet, I was brought outside and given first aid by the ambulance crews who had accompanied the police. My head was dressed in a ridiculously huge bandage that made me look like the Mister men's MR Bump. I did an interview on the spot with the anti-fascist "Hope not Hate", which went viral, before the police decided to arrest the victims. Plod, after doing nothing to stop the fascists attacking us in one of London's most CCTV-covered areas, although they were parked seconds away, now swooped into action arresting not only the incapacitated fascists strewn all over the garden, but also me and my partner, Bridget. Bridget was handcuffed to a bed in the hospital, and I was taken to a police station where after a few hours of repeating "no comment", I was eventually released and picked up by my daughter, Ashlene, and her husband, Gary. Eventually some of the fascists who attacked us were charged. I didn't attend the court, but I believe some of them were convicted. Although I no longer see eye-to-eye with many people who were there with us on that day, everyone, with one exception, fought bravely. This includes Alex Gordon and Mick Lynch (both of whom subsequently behaved appallingly, but defended others that day by blocking fascists getting into the pub). Likewise, Glen Hart and retired members, Mike Sargent and Ray Knight, stood their ground. One person whose actions were questionable was Eddie Dempsey, whose "hardman" image was well and truly spoiled as he ran into the pub at the first sign of trouble, and by his own admission only participated by lobbing glasses from a safe distance. Eddie went on to become the Assistant and then Senior Assistant General Secretary of the union: he no doubt has ambitions on the top job, if he isn't found out first. I think he would be disastrous for the union as his red/brown politics are very dangerous.

After the attack, both Bridget and I were inundated with get well wishes and statements of support from Britain, Ireland and even Europe, for which we were very grateful. Bridget became the third great love of my life, and though we are no longer together she will always be a great friend and comrade. One night, we were sitting in her flat when my mobile rang, I answered and asked, "Who is it?" The answer was "It's Jeremy Corbyn." My response was "Bollocks, who is it really?" Jeremy had to put his son Zack, who I knew, on the line to persuade me that it was really him. He spoke to me and Bridget, giving his solidarity; he had been a long-time anti-fascist himself, and this was a wonderful and really touching thing to do, and I will always remember his kindness.

After the attack, I went up and down England, Scotland and Wales to anti-fascist meetings. As coincidence would have it, one of my former AFA contacts was already organising left-wing football fans in "Football Lads and Lasses against Fascism" or FLAF for short. They have mobilised on several occasions sometimes having "vigorous debates" with the far right over political differences. What the attack on us showed was that fascists despise organised workers who are part of the socialist movement, and are prepared to physically attack us when we put out a different point of view to theirs. Ironic indeed when they always claim to be the "defenders of Free speech". History shows us that scapegoating minorities because of their religion, be that religion Jewish, Muslim, or Catholic, is only the start of the process. Inevitably fascists turn their anger on the workers movement, assassinating and imprisoning our leaders, and banning unions, to protect the wealth of their backers. I hope that their attack on us exposed their true nature and persuade people that "no passaran" is more than just a slogan to be repeated, but a necessity that must be defended, by all means at our disposal. Hitler himself acknowledged that, "only one thing could have broken our movement – if the adversary had understood its principle from the first day and had smashed, with the most extreme brutality, the nucleus of our new movement". Goebbels agreed, admitting, "if the enemy had known how weak we were, it would have reduced us to jelly... it would have crushed in blood the very beginning of our work". We have it then from the horses' mouths that we need to smash fascists before they get their paws on the reins of power, as they will not hesitate to smash us if they do.

29 CASH BACK

Meanwhile back at the ranch, Mick Cash beat off the challenge of Sean Hoyle with relative ease. I had made the mistake of coming out to support Cash openly, as at one point the race was looking quite close. Although I had serious issues with Cash, thinking that he was wishy washy and right-wing, he had proved that he could do the job of General Secretary after a fashion, and I just didn't believe that Hoyle was a credible candidate. I had been lobbied by various people to stand against Cash myself, and weighing up the options, I didn't think I could win, and also thought that the election was bound to become very fractious and further split the union's activists and membership. Cash also made overtures to me about me succeeding him when he retired, but I knew this was bullshit as we were poles apart politically and industrially, and he would support a right-wing candidate as his successor – probably his new best friend, Assistant General Secretary, Mick lynch. This reluctant support for Cash didn't play well amongst my natural support, who couldn't stand Cash and believed Hoyle to be a genuine principled socialist. Having seen his behaviour in the boardroom I didn't share this view. If I had known that the result was not in doubt, I would have stayed out of the whole thing, but of course I didn't have the benefit of hindsight at that time.

When Cash got re-elected, he quickly became a different animal. Any pretence of being a nice guy was jettisoned. Staff were victimised, with those who had not supported his re-election campaign by actively campaigning for him being driven out of their jobs. Neutrality, which is the correct posi-tion for unelected staff, was seen as disloyalty; most accepted large payoffs with gagging clauses attached in order to keep them from exposing his bullying. I now began to seriously re-gret his re-election and my support of it. If I could relive this period of time, I would have stood against Cash myself. Even though success would have been very unlikely, I would have done my best to steer the union in what I thought was the best direction.

When Cash was elected General Secretary and I moved up to fill the Senior Assistant General Secretary role, there was an election for the other (junior) Assistant General Secretary's role. This was contested by Alan Pottage of the organisation unit, Mick lynch, the Euro Star branch secretary and former national executive member, and John Tilley. Pottage was seen as the left candidate, Lynch as the centrist, and Tilley, in RMT terms, as being on the right. Lynch was elected. He worked hard and developed a reputation as a talented negotiator. He was also incrementally ingratiating himself with Cash, play-ing on the latter's ego by always agreeing with him and flat-tering him. It was quite obvious that he had ambitions for the top job, a fact that Hoyle and his supporters had seen straight away, and this is probably why they became such obvious en-emies. They often argued vociferously with each other at un-ion conferences and even the Annual General Meeting, where policy is decided by elected rank-and-file delegates every year.

I had a good working relationship with Lynch and even defended him on occasion from what I saw as undeserved at-tacks. A case in point is when Paul Jackson asked publicly on

Facebook whether he should stand against Lynch when his term expired (he was in the last 6 months of his 5-year period). I answered in no uncertain terms that he should not and many seem to think I inferred that Jackson was a careerist. He certainly thought this and put in a complaint against me to that effect. Looking back, this was a grave mistake as Lynch proved to be more right-wing and unprincipled than I could ever have imagined in my wildest dreams, but more of that later.

Meanwhile the toxicity in the boardroom was reaching boiling point, with the majority of executive now in open warfare with Cash, Lynch, and a small minority on the executive who supported him. I aligned with neither of the factions, basically because I saw them both as unprincipled collections of largely apolitical careerists. I had to sit in the boardroom, which became an arena where the rival groups would try to discredit their opponents at every opportunity, with the sniping often becoming personal and not about policy. It is probably appropriate to mention that Cash could only rely on two unwavering supporters – Eddie Dempsey and Steve Shaw – who were both to stand for many elected positions in the RMT, with Shaw being largely unsuccessful and Dempsey being very successful. You can judge for yourselves what motivated their slavish loyalty to Cash despite them both claiming to be far more left-wing than their leader, politically and industrially.

Dempsey would go out of his way to befriend me. As his name suggests, he is of Irish extraction and played on his republican heritage. The fact that he was a Millwall fan made me somewhat suspicious, but he won me over by supporting the left position in the boardroom when I was doing my agenda items. I later learnt that he would support whichever officer happened to be in the room at that time, as we all came in separately, and on only very rare occasions were the General Secretary, Senior Assistant General Secretary, and Assistant General Secretary in the boardroom together.

Funnily enough I was alerted to this fact by another executive member, who was to go on to be the RMT's first elected female president. There was no love lost between me and Michelle Rodgers, as she had been a personal friend of Pat Sikorski and was now a supporter of Hoyle. I have to say though she was quote honest, and usually tried to do the right thing as an executive member, even though she was capable of falling blindly into line with Hoyle upon occasion.

When he left the executive, Dempsey stood for a relief regional organiser's job against Glen Hart, and was duly elected. He was a great speaker and could motivate people, he also had a certain charm which won people over. I hate to admit it, but I was taken in by Dempsey and supported his election. He was later to totally betray me and reveal himself as the slippery careerist that Michelle Rodgers had warned me about.

30 MADAME PRESIDENT

In December 2018, the RMT elected its first woman president with a landslide victory over Cash loyalist, Steve Shaw, by 7,198 votes to Shaw's 4,598, on a 15.8 percent turnout.

Michelle Rodgers was a veteran RMT/NUR member of 30 years standing, and Manchester South branch secretary. Her campaign also emphasised "our rank-and-file members playing a full part in running our great Union with grass roots bottom-up philosophy". Michelle herself is on record as saying, "Our best means of winning change is through coordinated industrial action. RMT has a proud history of helping members organise to take action; as president, I'd ensure that any group of workers who wanted to take action to improve their conditions at work were supported and encouraged in doing that, rather than being dissuaded or held back."

I supported Michelle's campaign as I thought that we needed a woman in a senior union position to act as a role model, and encourage other women to come forward and fill the senior roles. As a union we didn't reflect the makeup of our membership, either in terms of sex or race, with both women and people of colour being massively underrepresented. This was not tokenism, as I also genuinely thought Michelle was the best candidate and had the best policies. In the initial stages of her presidency, Michelle did indeed attempt to live up to these lofty ideals. However, when Covid arrived, she was ground down by Cash and the union bureaucracy, with them eventually, in my opinion, running rings around her, by deliberately exaggerating the importance of the presidency in order to play on her insecurities and intimidate her into doing what they wanted. In the end, she was not strong enough to enact her strategy of rank-and-file power, and looked absolutely miserable and depressed by the end of her three-year presidential term.

31 COVID KILLS OFF ANY LINGERING PRETENCE THAT CASH OR LYNCH IS LEFT-WING

The Covid-19 pandemic began in 2019 and was to have devastating consequences all over the world, with Britain being no exception. In the year 2019-2020 there were 1.7 billion railway journeys, this crashed to 0.4 billion journeys in 2020-2021, climbing back over the billion-journey mark in 2021 -2022, and still did not reach pre-pandemic rates by 2022-2023, with 1.4 billion journeys recorded. Office of Rail and Road figures revealed that money raised through fares between April 2020 and March 2021 fell by a massive £8.6 billion pounds compared with the previous year, and only £1.8 billion were raised through ticket sales. Lockdowns accounted for this, with the number of passenger journeys dropping by 77.7% in 2020-21 compared with the previous year. The government response was to pump in funding, adding another six and a half billion pounds to the existing £10.4 billion they were already contributing to ensure that the private railway companies still made handsome profits. In total, the £16.9 billions of taxpayers' money was used to scaffold the privatised railway, which otherwise may well have folded.

The money was made available through the Emergency Measures Agreement (EMA) in March 2020 as a result of lockdown, and was bolstered by the Emergency Recovery Measures Agreement (ERMA) in September 2020. These were introduced to support privately-owned franchise operators and to stop them from suffering revenue loss during the pandemic.

£10.2 billion went to the private train operators, an extra £9 billion pounds, and £6.6 billion to Network Rail and the Core Valley Lines (CVL) in the Wales Valleys, which were public bodies. This was an increase of £1.4 billon. Therefore, for every pound given to the public sector rail industry 6.8 pounds were given to the privateers. This is exacerbated by the fact that private train operators spent £10.3 billion, £0.4 billion less than the previous year, while Network Rail spent £9.6 billion, which was a £1.2 billion increase. So whilst private companies were given taxpayers' money, much of which was given to their shareholders in dividends, the public sector Network Rail was deliberately, in relative terms, starved of cash

During this period, rail services were cut by a fifth as essential journeys still needed to be made, but many trains ran nearly empty. This didn't stop the train operating companies and the rolling stock companies that leased them the trains making bumper profits. Private rail companies made nearly £500 million in profits out of the crisis on UK railways in a year.

Under the EMAs, the government also paid the total lease charges for the trains to the rolling stock companies 'ROSCOs', who profited to the tune of £241 million in the same period. Disgracefully, the train operating companies shelled out £38 million in dividends to their shareholders, whilst workers risking their lives had a pay freeze. The rolling stock companies paid out £950 million to their shareholders. This is indeed "socialism for the rich and capitalism for the poor".

What was the RMT leadership's response to this absolute piss-take? Well, the union agreed to "collaborate" with government throughout the "National Emergency", not only co-operate, but collaborate with the class enemy. The leadership wrote to members via the RMT news stating, "The union has secured guarantees on safety, pay, pensions and jobs for many of you, but some of our members have been treated abysmally and we will continue to fight for your interests with every tool at our disposal". This was disguising the appalling deal that had been done, the freezing of wages and the calling-off of strike action and even ballots.

On June 15, 2021, the RMT leadership continued to partici-pate in the Rail Industry Recovery Group (RIRG) created by Bo-ris Johnson's Conservative government. The RMT agreed an Enabling Framework Agreement (EFA) with Network Rail and the train operating companies. The meaning of this agreement was clear and unambiguous – it was "to address efficiency and cost savings" and "rebuild and modernise" the railways. RIRG set in motion plans for rail workers to pay with their pay freez-es, and even their jobs, for the cost of the pandemic, while shareholders had bumper pay-outs at their expense.

This caused much disquiet amongst members, which necessitated a letter from Mick Lynch to members in June 2021, explaining that the union would continue to participate in the RIRG, despite "noting" that the Enabling Framework Agreement "has the objective of reducing the overall operat-ing costs of the railway as the Government wants to reduce its subsidy. This will affect the overall number of jobs, work-ing practices, roles and other arrangements". Lynch justified RMT participation in this by saying it would be easier to pro-tect members' interests by participating than not taking part.

In reality, the Enabling Framework Agreement signed by the RMT pledged to "specifically address the workforce reforms and staff cost challenges the rail industry is facing". This meant that the RMT attended working parties with rail bosses that sought to cut jobs, freeze wages, destroy pensions, and introduce even more flexible working, i.e., those left behind doing the jobs of people who have been gotten rid of.

The agreement sought to make up £2 billion a year due to the fall in revenue from fares during the pandemic. This is what all the rail unions signed up to:

1) A pay freeze: The current two-year pay freeze for all but the lowest-paid rail workers (on £24,000 or less) is set to be extended, with the agreement stating, "we will review the basis for future annual pay review discussions to take into consideration the longer-term affordability and sustainability of the rail industry". This is an absolutely breath-taking action by a union leadership who knew that private companies were still paying out hundreds of millions to shareholders but accepting wage freezes for members.

2) Redundancies: "The industry will require fewer, and in some cases changes to roles". This attack on jobs would lead to the setting up of an "industry-wide Special Voluntary Severance Scheme". A "recruitment freeze" and the stated aim of making any future roles multi-functional. Again, while hundreds of millions were being literally given to shareholders sitting at home, the union leadership had agreed to negotiate job losses and multi- skilling.

3) Sackings: If the required number of job cuts had not been made, proposals even threatened compulsory redun-

dancies, which was a red line for the unions. The agreement was again explicit, stating that, "By no later than the end of 2021, if there is not sufficient evidence of progress or if discussions break down, the proposed employee support measures in this agreement will be amended or withdrawn". The union leadership had allowed the bosses to put a gun to their head, threatening compulsory redundancies unless they got their way with multi-skilling, redundancies, and other demands.

4) Incredibly the RMT leadership agreed a "Mutual Respect Code" with the bosses, agreeing to "support each other" if they came under pressure. What's worse, all this was to be kept from the members with all parties agreeing to a confidentiality clause "including confidentiality over dissemination of any relevant information that is shared, notwithstanding, that it is understood that all parties will need to periodically report on progress to their executive committees/boards and to key stakeholders including DfT and relevant government departments, TPR and the RPS Trustee". This notably does not include the 78,000 members of the RMT. It was in fact a deliberate attempt to keep RMT members in the dark to the true machinations that were being conducted behind their back by the union leaders and the government.

What is even more astounding than the RMT leadership agreeing to participate in this farce is the fact that there was practically no criticism from the rank-and-file activists, and only very muted and caveated criticism from the so-called left groups, who seemed to have absolutely no strategy but to fall in, in some cases begrudgingly, behind the leadership.

I personally became extremely frustrated by trade unionists, who sought to boast about their socialist credentials at every opportunity, lining up with the bosses in some fictional "national interest". To me at least the "national interest " in a capitalist country is simply the interests of big business and the ruling class, and is never the interests of the workers. The fact that so-called revolutionary socialists, although they agreed with my analysis in theory, went against it in practice exposes them as frauds and charlatans in my eyes. They are like the social democrats, who before the first world war called for international brother and sisterhood and the overthrow of bosses internationally, but then lined up like good little soldiers to support their own ruling class in 1914. It wouldn't have been rocket science to explain to RMT members, who had risked their lives to keep the country running during the pandemic, why they needed to fight a pay freeze, when hundreds of millions were being paid in dividends to shareholders sitting at home taking no risks during the Covid crisis.

32 BORIS JOHNSON AND HIS PART IN MY DOWNFALL

During the whole Covid period, I had become increasingly frustrated at the union's policy, which to me was little short of capitulation in front of the class enemy. I was totally isolated in the RMT boardroom, with the exception of one person who was a Socialist Party member, Jared Wood, who would sometimes take a class-conscious view of events. Jared was almost completely ineffective as an executive member, and seemed more interested in detailing the Socialist Party's position, in case there was criticism from other sects, rather than winning over other executive members to an alternative course of action. The rest of the leadership were absolutely incapable of coming to terms with the pandemic , seeming to have neither the will nor the political understanding to oppose the General Secretary's strategy of collaborating with the Boris Johnson government in regard to their railway policy. Instead, they meekly fell into line like so many startled rabbits caught in the headlights, prepared to follow any lead, as long as it meant they didn't have to lead themselves.

This situation was exacerbated by the executive agreeing to work remotely from their houses, and not even having the opportunity to engage in the usual boardroom debates, where they could at least listen to different points of view. Instead, everyone was now operating on Zoom from the safety of their living rooms, while the vast majority of our members were still at work, risking their safety to keep transport moving. Absolutely none of the leadership (save the aforementioned

S.P. member) was prepared to even countenance alternative strategies that I was putting forward.

My increasing frustration and sense of absolute powerlessness led me to going on Facebook at nights, often having consumed too much alcohol. I was responding to a thread about Boris Johnson having the Corona virus and wrote "Yes, poor virus. I hope the whole cabinet of Tory b******s get it too. I don't want to offend you, but if Bojo pops his clogs I'm throwing a party. I hope the whole cabinet and higher echelons of the Tory party have been touching various bits of him".

I hate Boris Johnson and everything he represents, his privilege and class snobbery towards working-class people are well documented, and contain some appalling classist statements Johnson made over decades. This is hardly surprising from a former member of the Bullingdon club, a private all-male Oxford University outfit, famous for its wealthy members, ostentatious shows of wealth, vandalism of restaurants and students' rooms. Imagine if this behaviour was replicated by a lot of black, Asian, or white working-class youths in East Ham, and you can quickly ascertain that classism is alive and well in 21st century Britain. New members of the Club have to burn a £50 note in front of a beggar as part of an "initiation ceremony" it has been claimed in an Oxford student newspaper. Former Prime Minister, David Cameron, was also a member.

Johnson's hatred of the working class is apparent in his various vacuous scribblings. In 1995, writing for the Spectator, he wrote "Working-class men are likely to be drunk, criminal, aimless, feckless & hopeless. And perhaps claim to suffer from low self-esteem, brought on by unemployment". Over a decade later in 2007, writing in the Spectator commentating on working-class women, who chose or were forced through economic necessity to go to work, Boris wrote, "The result is that in families on lower incomes the women have absolutely no choice but to work, often with adverse consequences for family life and society as a whole – in that unloved and undisciplined children are more likely to become hoodies, NEETS, and mug you on the street corner".

Johnson was not only classist, he was also racist. In 2002, his racism was on display when he wrote in the Spectator, seemingly advocating a recolonisation of Africa to solve its problems, saying "The best fate for Africa would be if the old colonial powers, or their citizens, scrambled once again in her direction; on the understanding that this time they will not be asked to feel guilty". The same year he opined in the Telegraph on Blair's visit to the Congo, "No doubt the AK47s will fall silent, and the pangas will stop their hacking of human flesh, and the tribal warriors will all break out in watermelon smiles to see the big white chief touch down in his big white British taxpayer-funded bird". This is absolutely extraordinary behaviour for any politician, especially one who would have the arrogance to stand for prime minister, but Johnson was just warming up. In 2005, Johnson wrote this little gem of wisdom attacking a major religion in the Spectator magazine, "To any non-Muslim reader of the Koran, Islamophobia — fear of Islam — seems a natural reaction, and, indeed, exactly what that text is intended to provoke". Therefore we have a well-known politician normalising the fear of Islam when extreme right-wing groups all over the world were using strategy. Indeed, in Britain the fascist BNP gained nearly 200,00 votes in local elections in the same year.

In 2008, as editor of the Spectator, Johnson allowed an article claiming that "Orientals...have larger brains and higher IQ scores, blacks are at the other pole". This again is extraordinary. It is the editor's job to make sure any articles in a magazine are balanced and do not cause unnecessary offence. The article which claims black people have smaller brains is not only a patent lie, but is also explicitly racist. Either Johnson was asleep at the wheel as editor or more likely found this claptrap acceptable.

2010 saw him at it again, writing: "It is said that the Queen has come to love the Commonwealth, partly because it supplies her with regular cheering crowds of flag-waving piccaninnies". There is now a clear pattern of Johnson using the most offensive stereotypes of black people repeatedly in his articles. This is building a profile of an influential and privileged politician, who is both racist and classist, repeatedly attacking those less fortunate and less powerful than himself. They are, in my view, the actions of a bully, which would not be tolerated from someone who was not wealthy, powerful and upper middle- class.

His racism is still evident in 2018, less than a year before becoming prime minister. Writing for *The Telegraph* about a burqa ban, he said that it was "absolutely ridiculous" that "people should choose to go around looking like letter boxes".

Not content with classist and racist comments, Johnson had also turned his fire on gay people. In 1998 when Peter Mandelson resigned, Johnson wrote about "Tanked topped bum boys in the ministry of sound crying into their pils". In his 2001 book, "Friends, Voters, Countrymen," Boris wrote, "If gay marriage was OK – and I was uncertain on the issue – then I saw no reason in principle why a union should not be consecrated between three men, as well as two men, or indeed three men and a dog." So, in his eyes presumably, being gay was equivalent to bestiality.

Then there is his appalling record with misogyny. Speaking about Kimberly Quinn, then the publisher of the Spectator magazine, Boris said, "Relax. It's only Kimberly, with some helpful suggestions for boosting circulation. Just pat her on the bottom and send her on her way." In 1996, in the Telegraph under the headline "Hot Totty is on the agenda as women start to scent victory", he wrote, "The unanimous opinion is that what has been called the 'Tottymeter' reading is higher than at any Labour party conference in living memory. Time and again the Tottymeter has gone off as a young woman delegate mounts the rostrum."

When he became prime minister, there were also allegations of women being patronised and treated less favourably than men. With England's only woman Metro mayor, Tracy Brabin, claiming he allowed a "wild west" culture of misogyny in Westminster by permitting "the arrogance of privately educated men," to create a misogynistic culture in government. In June 2022, responding to an ITV documentary on the subject, Downing Street has admitted that there was a "nasty, misogynist culture" under Boris Johnson's premiership.

Responding to an ITV documentary containing fresh revelations about his leadership, Guto Harri, Downing street's director of communications, admitted that such a toxic culture persisted, but blamed it on Boris's aides claiming, "Previous aides who have devoted their lives to bringing down the PM did indeed preside over a nasty, misogynist culture".

It beggars belief what Britain's "free and impartial press" would have done if Jeremy Corbyn or any other left politician had uttered or written even a smidgen of the absolute hate speech and venomous writings that dripped from Johnson's pen and tongue in equal measures. The hacks in Fleet street and the presenters in the employ of billionaire TV owners were aided and abetted by the bastion of the establishment, the BBC in minimising the shocking racism, sexism, and homophobia of Johnson, whilst simultaneously tarring Jeremy Corbyn as an antisemite, without so much as a shred of evidence. If this is a free press, I dread to see what the definition of a controlled and partial press entails.

To top it all off, it is now known that Boris was the one actually doing the partying, whilst everyone else was obeying the lockdown restrictions, meaning that they couldn't attend hospitals, care homes or even funerals to see or say farewell to relatives. Johnson who had made the rules was pissing it up with his cohort, who obviously thought they were above the law. His constant denials that he had attended parties, and the subsequent facts emerging that he had indeed been present, led to a series of resignations by senior and junior government ministers, forcing Boris himself to finally resign, and effectively be dragged kicking and screaming from office on 8th July 2022. He finally resigned as an MP on 10th June 2023 before a Commons investigation into whether he misled Parliament over partygate reported back, claiming the report's authors, the majority of them conservatives, were attempting to "drive me out".

The inquiry concluded that Johnson knowingly misled parliament several times with his statements about parties in Downing Street during the Covid pandemic.

The Privileges Committee recommended a suspension of 90 days if he were still an MP, which could have triggered a byelection. MPs voted overwhelmingly to back the report into his misbehaviour with just seven MPs voting against the Privileges Committee's findings.

All in all, Johnson is a nasty racist, Islamophobic, classicist, misogynist piece of work and I will shed no tears when he shuffles off this mortal coil. I do accept though that my comments during Covid were completely ill-timed and may have offended many people whose friends, or loved ones suffered from the terrible disease, and may even have lost their lives. For causing this offence I am truly sorry.

33 I AM SUSPENDED

On being informed of my Facebook comments, Mick Cash, the RMT General Secretary, phoned me complaining that he had been contacted by the Sun newspaper (a rag hated by any self-respecting trade unionist) and asked to comment. I replied, "What are you doing talking to the Sun?" and admitted that I had made the comments. Cash then convened a national executive meeting on Good Friday, 10th April 2020, without my knowledge (I should have been invited) which suspended me. Cash and the president, Rodgers, then issued a joint statement to the press without informing me, saying that I had been suspended and that "Steve Hedley's comments do not represent the views of this trade union and are wholly unacceptable."

Without getting any chance to defend myself, I was stripped of my Senior Assistant General Secretary's title, and was somehow now the junior although I'd been in the post the longest.

In the meantime, Cash had completely fallen out with the vast majority on the national executive committee, refusing to meet with them and then issuing an email to the entire membership, accusing them of bullying before he fell sick with mental health issues. This meant that Mick lynch who had been promoted to Senior Assistant General Secretary due to my demotion took charge of the union. Lynch followed Cash's example in a matter of weeks himself, going off sick claiming mental illness, and emailing all members attacking the majority of national executive as bullies, even naming individuals who he claimed were bullying him.

I cannot stress enough how inappropriate this behaviour was. The General Secretary and his assistants do not make decisions for the union, their role is to carry out the decisions of the national executive. Of course, the General Secretary is influential and can attempt to persuade the executive to take a different course of action, but ultimately the executive are in charge. This is spelled out crystal clear in the RMT rulebook. If by their own admission the General Secretary cannot persuade the majority of the national executive, they must carry out the executive's decision. To claim that this is bullying is absolutely absurd.

With no national officer left, I had to step in and take control of the union, acting as the General Secretary. I was in this position for a couple of months and tried my best to heal the wounds in the union. One thing I did almost immediately was to reinstate a long-time employee of the union, who had been sacked, in what was in my opinion a shocking decision by the union leadership, and would have brought disgrace on the RMT if it had become public knowledge. When the news reached Cash that I was standing in as General Secretary and reinstating sacked employees, he seemed to miraculously recover from his ailments and came back to work. He remained at loggerheads with the national executive right up until the 2020 Annual General Meeting of the union.

At the 2020 Annual General Meeting, which was delayed until November, my appeal against my suspension and demotion was heard. Delegates knew that part of the reason for my harsh treatment was that I opposed the 'national unity' arguments of the leadership during Covid, and had argued against the leadership calling off strikes. I had taken the minority position that we should continue our action as the bosses of the railway companies were being bailed out by the government (in reality the taxpayer), enabling them to shell out hundreds of millions to shareholders, whilst enforcing a pay freeze on workers.

Many delegates spoke in support of me, absolutely aghast at the lack of due process that had been followed, and accepted the apology that I had made to them and the membership for my actions. When I got the chance to speak, I laid into Mick Cash for capitulating to the capitalist press, for standing against a true leader in Bob Crow, for usurping the unions power by failing to follow the directions of the NEC, but instead refusing to even meet with them. For failing to uphold the agreed union democracy and for failing to oppose the war in Iraq. These things, I argued, brought the union into disrepute far more than my comments about Johnson.

Mick Cash responded demanding delegates vote against the appeal, or he would stand down from his position as General Secretary. The delegates called his bluff by supporting the appeal with 44 for and 23 against. Cash then, in an obviously choreographed display, announced that he was retiring, not resigning but retiring, which would allow him to oversee the election of his successor, and to promote his favourite candidate, a promotion that would start that very day at the AGM.

Almost immediately, an online report announcing the General Secretary's retirement was retweeted by RMT head office, showing that this was pre-planned, and attacking the delegates to the AGM, the rank-and-file of the union, and blaming them for bullying and factionalism.

This disgraceful behaviour from Cash, after a democratic decision from the union's supreme bodyduring which the AGM had failed to be blackmailed by his threat of resignation, followed a series of letters from the General Secretary to the membership attacking the RMT national executive committee. Cash obviously believed that his position as General Secretary put him above the union's democratic structures. He was very wrong.

Cash said that he would not go immediately, but would oversee the election of his successor. Having attacked me throughout the AGM, he did his best to promote Mick Lynch, even hugging him in front of the delegates, and saying what a great support he had been during Cash's period of mental illness. Lynch had himself gone off sick claiming that he was mentally ill too, but not before accusing the majority of the national executive committee of bullying. This narrative of the brave General Secretary, Cash, and his trusty assistant, Lynch, standing up to bullies and being made ill in the process was propagated by the leadership, the union's right wing, and the so-called "broad left" (a Communist Party /Labour Party /right wing of the RMT lash-up). Their story was absolute nonsense, and the reverse of what had actually happened, but unfortunately it was believed by the majority of the membership, as several emails to all members had propagated this nonsense.

Also, during the AGM when Cash was speaking, I had scratched my head for literally two seconds at most; this led to allegations by Cash's supporters that I was somehow mocking his mental illness. Several almost identical complaints went in within minutes of each other the next day, including from the founder of the broad left, Communist Party member, and soon to be president of the union, Alex Gordon. Reading the complaints and their remarkable similarities I was reminded of a load of kids who had copied each other's homework. Considering that the meeting was on Zoom, I was supposed to believe that seven people, all Mick Cash supporters, had spotted me "touching my head" and interpreted this as mocking Cash's mental illness. This was clearly in my view, a pre-planned and coordinated attack on me to sabotage any election campaign I might launch for the soon to be vacant General Secretary's position.

To say that the hearing I had was biased is an understatement. Alex Gordon, who had been elected president, was part of the committee who had decided to discipline me despite him also having put in a complaint against me on that very subject. No trade unionists anywhere would accept this ridiculous situation when dealing with an employer, when a boss who actually made a complaint would sit on a committee to also process and deal with the same complaint – there isn't even the pretence of any independence in this situation.

34 THE GENERAL SECRETARY ELECTION

I knew that my chance of winning the election for the General Secretary's position was an extremely long shot. The right wing and the broad left were rallying around Lynch, who Cash had done his best to anoint as his successor at the 2020 AGM. There were also another two candidates who would split the lefty vote: John leach, the London Transport regional organiser (supported by the AWL, of which his partner was a leading member, an organisation who wanted to decriminalise digital child porn) and Scottish Regional Organiser, Gordon Martin, who was obviously not someone who could win a UK-wide ballot. Added to this was what I considered an obvious smear campaign run by Alex Gordon and those who had put in complaints against me. (I had met Alex Gordon 25 years previously when he was an anarchist. Later he became a Trotskyist before discovering around the age of 50 that he was a communist and joining the Communist Party, which was coincidentally very influential in the RMT.) I nevertheless was determined to use the campaign, which mainly consisted of Zoom meetings, because we were still in the Pandemic, to expose what had really happened in the union and how Cash and Lynch, in my opinion, had attempted to undermine the democratic structures of the union by seeking to not only undermine the elected national executive committee, but, in the case of Cash, to even prevent them meeting by refusing to convene meetings.

As predicted, Lynch picked up the vast majority of branch nominations. At Paddington's closed branch, they didn't allow any visitors that night, contrary to RMT rules. In the meeting, Eddie Dempsey, who had pretended to be a friend of mine, nominated Mick Lynch for the General Secretary's position. Candidates were not allowed to attend and speak to members or answer their questions. This practice of branch officers steering the membership was unfortunately not an isolated incident and may have contributed to the fact that less than one in five members cast their ballot in the election. The turnout, as usual, was very poor, with only 19.4% of union members participating in the ballot. Lynch won 7,605 votes, I got 4,352 votes, Leach 2,944 votes and Martin 1,628 votes. The combined "left vote" would have defeated Lynch, but of course there is no guarantee that all these votes would have transferred to any one left candidate.

I had not held back at the various hustings, and spoke honestly about how I thought Cash and Lynch had totally ignored the established democracy of the union in order to get their own way. I knew that this would have consequences for me, but had come to the end of my tether, and didn't think I could spend another five years sitting silently as the union I loved was turned into just another toothless Labour Party fan club. I reasoned that if I stayed in the leadership of the union, then I was bound by the collective responsibility that was inherent in such a position, and couldn't publicly criticise even the decisions that I thought were cowardly and would have terrible consequences for our members and the wider working-class. If I ended up getting driven out, then at least I could criticise the rightward drift of the union and in this way be better positioned to counter the right wing.

35 THE RMT "BROAD LEFT" AND THE ELECTION OF ALEX GORDON AS RMT PRESIDENT

The RMT broad left was formed in January 2020. Initially, I have to admit that I thought it sounded like a very good initiative and was even tempted to join.

It was formed to "defend and promote our union's objective for the supersession of the capitalist system by a socialistic order of society", to be brought about "through nationalisation and democratic ownership of the means of production, distribution and exchange".

I should have, however, spotted the real reason for its creation, as they promised not to "undermine RMT's democratically elected leaders but reserves the right to criticise our union leadership in a spirit of constructive engagement with the aim to strengthen our union". What this meant in reality was that there would be slavish support for the leadership and the right wing in an electoral pact in the union, the quid pro quo being that the right wing would then support broad left candidates like Communist Party member, Alex Gordon, who stood for President, and Eddie Dempsey who would stand for the Assistant General Secretary position. It proved a very good strategy for the broad left. When Lynch was elected as General Secretary, he left a vacancy for Assistant General Secretary, which Dempsey stood for. He was elected in October 2021 to serve a five-year term until October 2026. Dempsey beat the very experienced and, in my opinion, far better candidate, Alan Pottage, who had a track record of organising and recruiting thousands of workers into the union as head of the organising unit. Although I didn't think Alan would be suitable for the top job, I think he would have made an excellent Assistant.

Gordon was elected president in 2021 to serve a three-year term beginning in 2022. He had previously held the position from 2010-2012. Gordon defeated Sean Hoyle on a very poor turnout of members votes, and immediately set about ingratiating himself even further with Lynch and the right wing of the union.

36 PETRIT MIHAJ IS SACKED, AND THE ENTIRE RMT LEADERSHIP CROSS HIS PICKET LINE

Petrit Mihaj was a rep in the catering company Sodexho, who were sub-contractors for London Underground. He was actually a supervisor, but risked his job to take up the RMT reps' position and recruited nearly all his workmates into the union. This was no mean feat, as many of the Sodexho staff were immigrant workers who were very intimidated by their management, and up until that point had been afraid to join the union.

Needless to say, Petrit, himself an immigrant from Albania, was absolutely fearless in demanding that the company treat their workers with respect, as unfortunately casual racism and sexism were rife. Obviously, with a vicious anti-union employer, this organising ability put a target on Petrit's back and some management stooges manufactured an argument with him. When he responded they put in a complaint that he was bullying them and got him sacked. A yearlong campaign, including pickets and occupations of Sodexo offices, was ultimately unsuccessful in securing his re-instatement.

Petrit then got a job with the RMT union learning fund and again was very industrious and successful in his new role, organising courses for workers in subjects such as basic Maths and English, and then developing people, allowing them to progress in their education and their careers. The union learning fund was finally wound up and Petrit was made compulsorily redundant by then General Secretary, Mick

Cash. This was an outrage as the RMT had a policy of no compulsory redundancies, and although the union learning fund was not strictly part of the union itself, Petrit had worked with the RMT for nearly seven years. If an employer had behaved in this way, no trade unionist would have accepted it. How could we argue that employers should not make people compulsorily redundant when the union leadership were doing the same thing?

Petrit was not prepared to accept what he saw as completely unfair treatment, brought about, he was certain, by his refusal to support Cash's re-election campaign when he ultimately retained the General Secretary's job. He pointed to examples of people who had supported Cash being found jobs, and was livid that whilst he was being made redundant, people, including Alex Gordon's partner, Sarah Friday were given jobs with the union during the same period. Petrit saw this as a slap in the face and complete hypocrisy from the union leadership. He responded to the situation by initiating talks with the new General Secretary, Mick Lynch, to try and get his job back. When this strategy proved unsuccessful, he set up a picket outside the union headquarters.

I remember Petrit's picket very well, as I was running late due to train delays and arrived at about 9.30 am at the office. I was shocked that the RMT were being picketed and I went over to the pickets to get an explanation. I was actually supposed to meet Mick Lynch that morning at 10 am, but as there was a picket, I of course couldn't cross it and instead went to sit in a café across the street, where another two members of staff who had also refused to cross the picket were already having breakfast. I phoned Lynch to find that he was already in the office and asked him to go and speak to the pickets and resolve this shameful situation so that I and the other staff could get into work. To his credit Lynch, on this occasion, did discuss matters with the pickets and a few days later reinstated Petrit. I was delighted that the situation had seemingly been resolved amicably, but was to be left bitterly disappointed by Lynch's subsequent actions.

Having reinstated Petrit, Lynch almost immediately suspended him again and ultimately sacked him, saying that he was no longer redundant, but dismissed, and now had to pay the union back the redundancy money that had been paid into his bank account. To me this was behaviour that I would never have believed possible from the RMT leadership. We were a worker's organisation that had a national and indeed international reputation of fiercely defending workers' rights and were behaving as badly as any boss that I'd ever seen.

Petrit had even won his appeal against being made compulsorily redundant at the union's Annual General Meeting, the supreme governing body of the union, and this decision incredibly was met by the staff walking out. The president, Rodgers, could have continued with the AGM, but instead closed it down without the minutes being agreed. This allowed the General Secretary to ludicrously overturn union policy by saying that despite a democratic vote in Petrit's favour, because the minutes hadn't been ratified then the decision couldn't be implemented. This was a very selective interpretation as it wasn't applied to any other decision where the minutes hadn't been formally agreed.

Infuriated by these scandalous bureaucratic manoeuvres, Petrit again resorted to picketing the RMT head office. I was actually shaken to my core when not only Lynch, Dempsey and Gordon crossed his picket, but also the entire executive of the RMT. Some of the scabs were in the Socialist Party and I was astounded that they had followed suit. These people were not naïve workers new to industrial action, but veterans of many struggles. Some of the scabs were indeed historians of the workers' movement, who knew exactly the betrayal that they were committing of everything the working-class and trade union movement stood for. The one unbreakable rule of trade unionism is that you do not ever, no matter what the circumstances, cross a picket. To cross a picket is to become a scab to quote Jack London

"After God had finished the rattlesnake, the toad, and the vampire, He had some awful substance left with which He made a scab. A scab is a two-legged animal with a corkscrew soul, a waterlogged brain, and a combination backbone made of jelly and glue. Where others have hearts, he carries a tumour of rotten principles."

London's piece was often quoted by the very people who had themselves now crossed a picket. The role of shame was added to by John Leach (supported by the AWL), the London Transport regional organiser, who seemed to benefit from his actions when I retired, by standing completely unopposed by anyone, including his enemies in the Socialist Party for the position of Assistant General Secretary. In a completely co-incidental event, Jared Wood of the Socialist Party stood for Leach's old position, again completely unopposed (no AWL candidate standing against their bitter opponents for some reason).

This absolutely brazen and rotten behaviour by people who called themselves revolutionary socialists and even communists, actually provoked a kind of personal crisis in me. I seriously wondered if I had lived a complete lie in the 33 years that I had been an RMT member. I would never have believed in a million years that these people would have crossed a sacked worker's picket, knowing full well that a worker has the legal right to picket a workplace from where they've been sacked, while pretending that it wasn't in fact a picket, but just a protest, in order to justify their treachery to the most sacred of working-class principles ,the 11th commandment, "thou shalt not cross a picket line".

37 I RETIRE FROM THE RMT

In the end I was the only person who would not cross the picket line. After months of picketing, I knew that they were not going to win, but that was no excuse to betray every principle that I believed in. I had asked the pickets if they thought it was okay if I worked from home and they agreed that this was fine. My enemies will obviously try and use this against me, but I was careful to clear it with the pickets before I joined Zoom meetings including the NEC meetings. These meetings had previously been conducted on Zoom for months, but now that there was a picket, the leadership had instructed everyone to attend in person. I considered this an attempt to make everyone including me cross the picket, and point blank refused to do so.

My position was now untenable, made more so by the General Secretary's instruction that we had to physically come into work, and in doing so cross the picket. All this was wreaking havoc with my mental health. I had seen the RMT as not just the best union in Britain and bastion of defending workers' rights, but also as a vehicle for a truly socialist society. Having seen everything that I had believed the union stood for turned on its head and betrayed by the leadership, I became depressed with the whole situation. I became uncommunicative and, thinking that no resolution was possible, was even contemplating suicide. I do not write about this lightly, but feel that it is necessary to understand the toll that this awful betrayal of every decent working-class principle by the RMT leadership had taken on me personally.

I discussed the situation with family members who had noticed the changes in my behaviour, going from confident, talkative, and sometimes boisterous, to withdrawn and anxious. It took my ex-wife to come up with the obvious solution. She said, "it's not the same RMT that you joined, don't feel guilty, you need to move on and do something else". A few days later, I contacted my Branch Secretary, Paul Jackson, who negotiated my retirement on medical grounds. In addition to my mental health issues, I had also badly injured my right knee, rupturing the meniscus, and was having trouble walking long distances. Like any worker, I took some money from the deal, but only what I was entitled to and not the life-changing sums my enemies bandied about to discredit me. I was also referred to "talking therapy" during this time, which was done over the phone and proved to be absolutely no help at all. It took me nearly a year to fully recover mentally, removing myself from the toxic atmosphere of the RMT head office was the beginning of me getting better.

I am absolutely amazed that in the middle of the biggest railway strike in thirty years when Mick Lynch was attending picket lines all over the country, and simultaneously crossing the picket outside his own office of a worker he'd sacked, that not one member of the right-wing press questioned him on his behaviour. Did no one from the Sun or Murdoch's other appendages think of asking "isn't you crossing a picket a tad hypocritical Mr Lynch when you're asking workers throughout Britain not to cross pickets?" I ask you, the reader, to imagine the reaction of the press if I had have crossed a picket line in any circumstances, especially during a massive rail strike. Every tabloid redtop would have screamed "scab" and "hypocrite", and to be honest with some justification. Why then was Lynch treated with kid gloves just at the time when Murdoch's henchmen could have put the boot in?

What is equally astounding is the free pass given to Lynch by the so-called left papers, the Morning Star, the Socialist, the Socialist Worker, and whatever rag the AWL now have. None of these exposed the "working-class hero" for being exactly what they all knew he was, an absolute scab. Petrit had recorded the RMT leadership crossing picket lines and distributed several videos throughout the trade union and socialist movements so they can't use the excuse of "they didn't know". They knew all right and to their eternal shame they sided with the oppressor and not the oppressed. What are the reasons for this? Well, there may be a combination of excuses. Perhaps the "comrades" were bought off by positions (after all Communist Party members, Socialist Party members and the AWL- supported Leach also scabbed) within the union or were afraid that union funding to their various front organisations would dry up. Perhaps it was just cowardice that prevented them from speaking up against the leadership's appalling behaviour, or perhaps it was a combination of all the above. Whatever the reasons were, it exposed the absolute uselessness of almost the entire British left, who proved that they would rather, when push came to shove, side with a right-wing bureaucracy, rather than with a sacked worker. In my opinion, they are an absolute disgrace to the name of socialism, and I cannot take seriously anything they say ever again. I haven't found even one tiny left sect who were prepared to take up Petrit's case and stand up for a worker against the union bureaucrats.

The only exception to the total lack of coverage of the appalling behaviour of the RMT leadership bureaucrats came from an independent journalist, David Lear. David had met Petrit when he was sacked from Sodexo and covered the protests outside their head office. When Petrit contacted him again, he spent weeks outside RMT headquarters, enduring verbal and even physical abuse to record attacks on the picket, including their placards being kicked over, stolen, and destroyed. It seems that David, and an honourable few, are what is left of the so-called "free press" in Britain. David told Petrit that his NUJ card was withdrawn because of his activities. This latest outrage added to the strange series of events already described begs the question "just what the hell is going on?"

The whole Petrit saga reached its appalling conclusion when he and four of his supporters, Mark Harding, Carol Foster (a retired member), Natasha Porter, and Peter Woods, were expelled from the RMT for refusing to stop picketing despite national executive instructions to do so. All of those expelled had a long and proud history of trade union activity and refused to be browbeaten into abandoning trade union principles. This took a lot of guts, as many who had initially supported Petrit, shied away when the union leadership began to crack down on his supporters. I have never previously heard of a case when a union executive all crossed a picket line, and then expelled its participants for refusing to stop picketing. This, in my opinion, shows the appalling state of the RMT's current leadership. The decision was endorsed by the union's Annual General Meeting, which didn't even have all those expelled present to be able to defend themselves. Had the AGM been in full possession of the facts, then I sincerely hope that a very different decision may have been reached.

After a period under the leadership of Bob Crow, where the RMT was a potential threat to the state and clearly a leading force on the left, both industrially and politically, this radicalness has effectively been neutralised by those who succeeded Crow, i.e., Cash and then Lynch. Cash was not good in the media and was a poor public speaker, but was a decent negotiator and absolutely ruthless with opponents from the left. He brought the RMT very close to reaffiliation to Labour, successfully using Jeremy Corbyn's leadership to convince a lot of people including (I must shamefully admit me) to, temporarily at least, abandon the idea of a new workers party, and instead seek to support the left in the Labour Party. Cash of course was always far to the right of Corbyn, not a Blairite by any means, but an old Labour right winger. Lynch in many ways built on Cash's legacy, as politically there was little difference between them. Lynch described himself recently as a "Tax and spend" old labour socialist, which is interesting because when Crow was General Secretary ,Mick then identified as a "Menshevik" (the opponents of Lenin and the Bolsheviks in the Russian Social Democratic Labour party). Lynch is a good public speaker and very good in the media, giving the impression that he is left-wing by talking left, whilst often acting right. The ability to give the impression of being a radical, when in reality doing the opposite, is far more dangerous to the workers movement than being a straightforward right winger, as illusions are sewn in workers and then disputes defused.

There was a very slow build up to the Network Rail and train operating companies' disputes, the biggest rail disputes since the 1990s. The government used the cover of the Covid pandemic to attempt to make massive cuts in the railway industry, seeking to slash the rail budget by an enormous 2 billion a year, whilst attempting a similar act of butchery on London Transport. While inflation was running rampant at over 11%, the government offered Network Rail workers, who had already had a two-year pay freeze, a paltry 2% and potentially an extra 1% if job cuts were made. As if this was not bad enough, the government wanted to impoverish people after they retired by making massive savings by reforming the railway pension scheme and the Transport for London scheme (one of the few schemes based on percentages of the workers' final salary that remained intact.)

Government attacks led to a building up of pressure from RMT members, who now hadn't had a pay rise in 3 years, and who demanded action from the union's leadership. Pushed by the grass roots members, the RMT leadership began balloting every Network Rail member and every member on the train operating companies. There were thirteen companies, namely, Avanti West Coast, c2c, Chiltern Railways, Cross-country, East Midlands Railway Greater Anglia, GWR, LNER, Northern, South-eastern, South Western Railway, Trans Pennine Express and West Midlands Trains, which all delivered massive Yes votes. The total number of people who would take strike action was around 40,000. The first days for the coordinated action were set for 21st ,23rd and 25th June. When the signallers, engineers, caterers, on-train and station staff stuck together, the service was devastated, with managers running only very infrequent token services. About 80% of the network was affected (Scotland and Wales were to reach separate settlements with the union). In addition, London Underground workers also struck on the 21st June, having a huge impact on tube services and further disrupting travel. The coordinated action was off to a great start with workers seeing the power that they had to practically shut the railway network. The union leadership, however, did not make the most of the boost in morale that this created.

Instead of going into negotiations demanding a rise at least in line with inflation, the RMT leadership made a huge blunder by setting out their stall by asking for a 7% pay rise. This was at a time when inflation, Consumer Price Index (C.P.I.), was 11% and coming after a two year pay freeze. In fact, the Retail Price Index, (R.P.I) inflation, which wages are traditionally based on, was even worse. In 2020 it was 2.1%, a year later in 2022 it had increased to 2.9% and absolutely skyrocketed to 13.8% in 2022.Given these circumstances, it is incomprehensible why the union leadership set such a low base mark for negotiations. As already mentioned, the private railway companies had paid out hundreds of millions to their shareholders in dividends over this period. Surely what was good for the goose was good for the gander?

Network Rail managers also creamed in the money with CEO, Andrew Haines, paid £585,000 (nearly thirty times more than station staff on £20,000). In 2021, Chief Financial Officer, Jeremy Westlake, was paid £415,000. How the same people could credibly argue that workers should have a two year pay freeze followed by an in real terms below inflation pay cut is incredible.

More strikes were called in July and August 2022, which were joined by the Transport Salaried Staff Association (TSSA) and the drivers' union ASLEF. This seemed to be movement in the right direction. In order to beat a confrontational government, intent on picking a fight with the unions so that it could bring in more anti-union legislation, the strike movement needed to be broadened, bringing in not just rail unions but, health service workers, post office workers, teachers, lecturers, civil servants and bus workers, who were also in dispute.

The TUC would not coordinate the action, so it was down to trade union leaders who were actually in dispute. The RMT General Secretary, Lynch, began touring Britain with CWU leader, Dave Ward, under the "Enough is enough" campaign banner. There were five demands, which the campaign pushed, namely 1. A Real Pay Rise (at least in line with inflation). 2. Slash Energy Bills. 3. End Food Poverty. 4. Decent Homes for All. 5. Tax the Rich. Just how these aims were to be achieved without building towards a general strike was not explained, and in reality, it just became a platform for trade union bureaucrats to talk left whilst acting right. Eventually, both Lynch and Ward reached pay deals that broke the campaign's first aim when the RMT and CWU settled disputes for payments massively below rates of inflation, and therefore agreed real terms pay cuts.

On 13th July, the RMT called a fourth twenty-four-hour strike action after rejecting Network Rail's latest pay offer, which it rightly saw as the government "threatening to impose compulsory redundancies and unsafe cuts to maintenance work" if strike action was not withdrawn. ASLEF announced that train drivers at eight train companies – Arriva Rail London, Chiltern Railways, Great Western Railway, LNER, Greater Anglia, South-eastern, Hull Trains and West Midlands Trains – would strike on 30th July. This involved over 5,000 drivers. RMT coordinated strikes on Network Rail and 14 train operators on 18th and 20th August, the TSSA also took action on these dates. This again was certainly progress with the rail unions beginning to act together against the common enemy and potentially act as a beacon to other sections of workers who were already in struggle or in the process of balloting to taking action. On 30th July, 5,000 members of ASLEF at eight rail companies, including South-eastern and West Midlands Trains, went on strike. This again was very effective, virtually shutting the network and building the confidence of the strikers.

The TSSA had always been an unreliable ally and on 5th August 2022 their Network managers accepted a 4% pay rise, allowing Network Rail to run a minimal service. United action was exactly the tactic needed to negotiate an inflation pay deal. All the unions acting together proved to be devastating for managers trying to run a service, for once the union leaders had seemed to have put factional differences aside. The fact that the TSSA broke ranks after such an impressive strike was unfathomable and would give the government a propaganda victory saying, "if it's good enough for them why is it not good enough for you?" to the other unions.

The 18th August saw another RMT strike with Network Rail signal workers from England, Scotland and Wales also joining the industrial action. RMT members in London also planned a twenty-four hour strike action and this took place on 19th August, sandwiched between the Network Rail and TOC strikes. The TOCS and Network Rail workers continued action on the 20th which was very effective, once more massively disrupting rail services. It was becoming clear, however, that discontinuous action with a few days a month on strike was not putting the government under sufficient pressure to achieve pay rises that kept pace with inflation, or even seemed to force serious concessions from the bosses. It was obviously the time in the dispute where the union leaders needed to argue for more sustained action over longer periods. This may not have been an easy argument, but the leadership's job is to explain what is necessary to win, and argue for that position, rather than take the easy option and put on strikes that everyone can afford, but will not result in a significant improvement.

The RMT, ASLEF and the TSSA had all planned to have strikes in September 2022, but in a possibly crucial mistake, the leaderships called off the action to allow people to go and see the body of the Queen lying in state at Westminster. This capitulation to establishment manufactured "public opinion" was to lose momentum in the strikes, and I would argue contribute greatly to the well-below inflation pay deal that was reached by the RMT on Network Rail.

On 20th September, both the RMT and ASLEF unions announced a strike for 1st October, with ASLEF calling another strike for 5th October. The RMT strike announced another twenty-four-hour strike for the 8th October. On 1st October, around 54,000 workers from four trade unions – the RMT, ASLEF, the TSSA and Unite, were striking side by side and this was the most effective of the strikes so far. At this point, it seemed that the unions had regained the initiative which they surrendered by calling off the previous action for the Queen lying in state. The last scheduled strike was for the 8th October. There were no more strikes in the book for after that date, the RMT leadership were forced to re-ballot their members in line with the stipulations of the anti-union laws. Members had to decide whether they wanted to continue with the strikes by again taking part in the ballot which would require over a 50% participation and at least 40% of all those eligible, voting yes. Three more strike dates were called for November, on 3rd, 5th, and 7th. However, on 25st October, the RMT leadership announced the strike on the third would be called off and that it would be rescheduled for 9th November to allow the Royal British Legion to come and sell poppies. Why the RMT leadership called off a strike for this is a mystery. It wasn't even Remembrance Day itself which is the 11th November, but just a day when people decided that they were going to sell poppies. Why couldn't the poppy sellers reschedule for a non-strike day? The RMT leadership again surrendered the momentum built up in previous strikes in an attempt to appeal to "public opinion".

In Scotland, a strike of Scotrail members was called for the 10th October when members rejected a 5% offer from the company, describing it as a "kick in the teeth". On 22nd October, there was a very effective RMT strike at Avanti West Coast, resulting in many the cancellations and delays to services throughout the whole 24 hours of action.

In an absolutely shocking move, the 4th November saw the RMT leaders once again suspending the scheduled strikes. The excuse given was that there was to be "a period of intensive negotiations" with Network Rail and the train operating companies. This was an absolute kick in the teeth for the members who were not consulted either through their branches, nor on mass Zoom meetings before the leadership pulled the strikes. Nothing new seemed to have been gained in negotiations. The proffered explanation that there would now be "intensive negotiations" led to a backlash from members asking, "well what were they doing before watching breakfast TV?"

ASLEF meanwhile pressed ahead with action calling out around 9,500 train drivers at 12 train operators to strike on 26th November. A strike by London Overground workers, scheduled for 26th November, was also suspended while the union executive considered a fresh pay offer from management.

With the "intensive negotiations" having delivered absolutely nothing, the RMT leadership were forced to announce four 48-hour strikes in the run up to Christmas, and early 2023, with strike action scheduled for 13th –14th December 16th –17th December 3rd –4th January and 6th –7th January, the RMT leadership, having been criticised by their grass roots members also called a strike for all RMT members working for Network Rail. This was to take place over Christmas, starting at 18:00

on Christmas Eve and ending at 06:00m on 27th December. This would involve around 20,000 staff. This Network Rail action was really to target the engineering work that was scheduled over Christmas as no trains ran at this time anyway. The cancellation of pre-planned engineering work scheduled for a time when there would be a break in services would cost the company millions and would necessitate replanning the work and getting the possessions of track to carry out the work. Of course, that did not stop the press and the government pretending to be ignorant of that fact and attacking the union for "spoiling Christmas". ASLEF announced drivers at 15 train companies would strike on 5th January 2023, on the day between the two RMT strikes announced for 4th and 6th January.

Having sought to court public opinion by calling off strikes for poppy sellers, the Queen's wake and "intensive negotiations" annoying members and taking momentum out of the strike, the RMT leadership handed the government a propaganda coup on a plate. The right-wing media soon labelled Lynch "the Grinch who stole Christmas". Of course, the strikes were called to exert the maximum possible leverage on the employers and the government, and the unions hoped that they wouldn't have to go ahead, but it was obvious that the government were not in the mood to negotiate and would obviously accuse the unions of stopping people getting home for Christmas. It seems odd that a leadership whose strategy seemed to be to keep the public on side would then do something seemingly completely contrary by calling the Christmas action.

39 "REPUBLICANS" LOSE THE MOMENTUM BY CALLING OFF STRIKES FOR THE MONARCHY

It's important to consider the effects of the RMT calling off the scheduled strike on 8th September because of the death of the Queen. This was not for her state funeral but merely to allow people to travel on the Rail Network to come and see her coffin. I think this was a dreadful mistake and sought to play to royalist "public opinion" rather than pursue a worker's dispute. Once again, the leadership had put "national interests" before working-class interests. It particularly stuck in the craw as this happened just as the RMT General Secretary, Lynch, was talking up his Irish Republican credentials and claimed Irish socialist, trade unionist and leader of the 1916 rebellion, James Connolly, was his hero. Connolly absolutely despised the institution of monarchy.

Here is quite a lengthy quote from Connolly made in 1910 on the occasion of a royal visit by King George 5th to Ireland. It completely encapsulates his ideas on the royals, and he expressed similar sentiments right up until he was tied to a chair and murdered by forces of the crown in 1916.

"What is monarchy? From whence does it derive its sanction? What has been its gift to humanity? Monarchy is a survival of the tyranny imposed by the hand of greed and treachery upon the human race in the darkest and most ignorant days of our history. It derives its only sanction from the sword of the marauder, and the helplessness of the producer, and its gifts to humanity are unknown, save as they can be measured in the pernicious examples of triumphant and shameless iniquities.

Every class in society save royalty, and especially British royalty, has through some of its members contributed something to the elevation of the race. But neither in science, nor in art, nor in literature, nor in exploration, nor in mechanical invention, nor in humanising of laws, nor in any sphere of human activity has a representative of British royalty helped forward the moral, intellectual, or material improvement of mankind. But that royal family has opposed every forward move, fought every reform, persecuted every patriot, and intrigued against every good cause. Slandering every friend of the people, it has befriended every oppressor. Eulogised today by misguided clerics, it has been notorious in history for the revolting nature of its crimes. Murder, treachery, adultery, incest, theft, perjury – every crime known to man has been committed by someone or other of the race of monarchs from whom King George is proud to trace his descent".

Just how anyone who had paid any heed to what Connolly thought about British monarchs could even contemplate calling off strike action in order for people to come and abase themselves at the feet of a dead monarchy beggars belief. This was not working with the best elements of the British working-class to break people from their mystification of all things royal; on the contrary, it was an appeal to the lowest common denominator, a surrender to base jingoistic instincts and really in, my view, amounted to class treachery.

Just when the RMT leadership were putting an illusory "national interest' above the workers struggle, the UK government continued to conduct class war announcing plans to ensure "minimum service levels" during strikes, and by allowing agency workers to replace striking staff. On 11th July the House of Commons approved the Conduct of Employment Agencies and Employment Businesses (Amendment) Regulations 2022. On 11th July these measures would force unions to instruct a percentage of their own members to cross picket lines on strike days. Let's say, for example, the minimum service was ordered to be 50%, this would mean at least 50% of union members would be told to break their own strike and go to work. This is completely anathema to any decent trade unionist, but I am willing to wager that union leaders would indeed order their members to break strikes rather than have the unions assets seized and lose their big salaries (usually five times of those on minimum wages), company cars, and privileged lifestyles.

40 THE RMT LEADERS AGREE A BELOW INFLATION DEAL FOR NETWORK RAIL AND LEAVE THE TOC MEMBERS TO FIGHT ALONE

On 19th January 2023 the Rail Delivery Group made a fresh offer to the RMT, of 5% for 2022 and 4% for 2023, but this was conditional on job losses and changes to terms and condition, which would mean a massive increase in weekend and night work. The RMT said they were "considering" the offer, but rejected it early in February after consulting with reps and members.

This was despite the RMT leadership signing a "Dispute Resolution Agreement" with all train operating companies (there are 14 TOCs) in total. These "National Principles" specifically laid out the "Workforce Changes" path, including job cuts and changes to terms and conditions. Incredibly it agreed to multiskilling all station staff, accepting that Sundays would become part of the working week, and that instead of working at a given station, a member of staff could be used to cover a number of different station locations. A new pay structure for any on train staff joining after that date which was far worse than the existing pay and conditions package, effectively creating a two-tier work force. In a spectacular own goal, the RMT leadership tacitly accepted the Train Operating Companies' rights to close ticket offices. The union leadership itself acknowledged that "Whilst the RMT does not support TOCs proposals to conduct statutory public consultation on the closure or re-purposing of ticket offices, the RMT acknowledges that the TOCs have the authority to implement such changes to ticket office provision that may arise from that process".

The RMT membership were just not prepared to accept this absolute sell-out and 4th May, 2023, RMT members across every one of the 14 TOCs delivered a massive vote for strike action, this re-ballot was necessitated by the anti-union laws which stipulate that to continue action a new mandate must be achieved every six months. Members had shown a weak leadership that they would not pay for below inflation pay rises in jobs terms and conditions. The union was forced to put four new strikes in 16th, 18th, and 30th March, and 1st April.

Incredibly whilst members on the train operating companies were still prepared to fight, the leadership were preparing a deal that came nowhere near the rate of inflation for Network Rail. The leadership didn't even have the courage to either officially recommend acceptance or rejection of the deal, but instead put it out to the members as "a best and final offer" from Network Rail and warned of the necessity of multiple strikes to improve it. This in my opinion was a "clean hands" strategy from the leadership putting the blame on the members for accepting a deal well below the rate of inflation and therefore a real terms pay cut.

Network Rail RMT members including engineers and signalling staff voted by just over three to one in favour to accept the offer, a 5% deal for 2022 and a 4% deal for 2023 together with a consolidated bonus of 750 pounds. The vote was 76%-24% to accept the offer, with workers seeing no strategy to win. The tactics of calling a few days of strikes months apart had failed, and worker demoralisation helped to account for the margin of acceptance. The decision by the leadership not to recommend a rejection of the deal was a major factor in the train operating company members being left to fight alone. The signal workers are a very powerful grade of workers and the fact that they would now work as normal would mean any strikes going forward would not be so effective. Undoubtedly, the train operating members could cause widespread disruption, but could not achieve the virtual closing of the network which took place when they struck together with Network Rail colleagues. In any impartial view of the dispute as a whole, this was a disastrous decision by the leadership, effectively hanging the train operating company members out to dry. As this is being written, the train operating company members bravely fight on and striked on 20th, 22nd and 29th July. These strikes as predicted caused a lot of disruption and cancellations, but were not on the scale of the previous united action. Without a major rethink of strategy involving longer periods of action in coordination with other workers, and actively spreading disputes, it is difficult to see how the RMT leadership plan on winning the TOC disputes. Rather than change ineffective tactics, they seem content to keep putting on days with limited success. The leadership cannot be blind to the fact that this will demoralise the members taking action, who are losing money to little effect. Perhaps it is very aware of this and is allowing the inevitable outcome to unfold, so once again their hands are seen to be clean.

In May 2023, ASLEF settled disputes in Wales and Scotland, but renewed the mandate for action in England when members voted overwhelmingly for strike and action short of a strike. ASLEF instigated an overtime ban for a week from 31st July to 5th August and from 7th August to 12th August on all train operating companies in dispute.

41 THE PERIOD 2022-2023: A WASTED OPPORTUNITY

2022-23 saw a huge upsurge in workers taking strike action. Many people, particularly in the public sector, had suffered over a decade of real terms pay cuts before covid, wage freezes during the pandemic and galloping inflation in double digits when we emerged from the lockdowns. The real terms wage cuts in some instances were equivalent to 25-30% of people's salaries. The disparity in wages and inflation was the catalyst for much of the action, although other factors like vacancies caused by people leaving because they couldn't live on the wages paid, and the huge workload this left on those who remained, were also important. Representatives of nurses, junior doctors, ambulance drivers, other NHS workers, and even consultants were joined by teachers and civil servants, who warned that public services were collapsing due to underfunding. There were also localised disputes with bus workers and sanitation workers over similar issues, and all together the situation if handled correctly would have posed a major threat to an unpopular government that was stumbling from one crisis to another.

Anyone who has had experience of trade unions knows full well that the Trades Union Congress (TUC) were not going to coordinate the action of the striking workers, and that a general strike under the auspices of the TUC was a non-starter. The TUC are an organisation that promotes social partnership (class collaboration) and wants to be a part of a corporatist Britain. It certainly does not see its role as challenging the government, at most it organises demonstrations and marches that allow people to let off steam and achieve absolutely nothing. Given that the TUC was not the vehicle to coordinate different workers in struggle, the only chance of workers building the necessary links was either down to union leaders or grass roots workers coming together. If trade union leaders had cooperated and explicitly challenged the government's policy of enforcing real terms wage cuts in order to tackle inflation, they may well have rallied sufficient forces to have smashed the government policy. Inflation was being caused by profiteering companies, the hike in oil and gas prices, exacerbated by the war in the Ukraine, and the horrendous rise in food prices. (Food inflation was over 20%). Public sector pay having been depressed for a decade could not possibly be driving the rise in inflation. This was not the usual scenario when a surplus of money in people's pockets led to them buying unnecessary or even luxury goods which pushed prices up. On the contrary, the commodities that were fuelling the price rises were staples that everyone needed such as gas, electricity, and food. The fact that the union leaders, although sometimes individually pointing out these obvious truths, did not combine overtly to challenge the government's strategy, not just intellectually, but on the picket lines, is nothing short of a complete dereliction of duty on their part. Afraid of being seen as leading "a political dispute" and the effect that this would have on the sacred cow of "public opinion", they cowered behind the mantra of "it's a purely economic struggle, our members just want a pay rise" or a "square deal".

With the TUC, and individual union leaderships being incapable or unwilling to lead the necessary fightback, the only possible recourse was that rank-and-file workers in different unions would organise in their own unions to challenge their bureaucracies, as well as across unions, to be able to start coordinating struggles. In short there were no existing grass roots organisations that could fill this role, nor did any develop. Sometimes when there are no mass political organisations of the left, the groups that inhabit that space are reduced to producing propaganda, aimed at the most politically conscious workers, and trying to win them to a militant and ultimately revolutionary position. Even this educational process was neglected by the mainstream Brit left. They ignored the obvious dead-end strategy of Lynch and the RMT leadership, and more often acted as cheerleaders, even when appalling deals were done, and this helped to mask the fact that real terms pay cuts had in fact been agreed, as was the case with Network Rail. The one exception is a miniscule Trotskyist group called the Socialist Equality Party, whose analysis was good, but had no chance of attracting support with their call to leave unions and set up workers committees. Most workers, many on strike for the first time, would naturally look to their union for leadership in the first instance. When the leadership inevitably sells the workers short, the call needs to be for the formation of grass roots organisations within the unions, to challenge the bureaucrats, and ultimately take action independently of them. This is a feasible plan and miles away from calling on inexperienced strikers to abandon the unions and go about setting up a small rival organisation that will enjoy zero support from most workers, and would only lead to the best activists being sacked.

It is becoming apparent that neither union leaders nor grass roots workers have been able to take advantage of the strike wave to force the government to abandon their attacks on the entire working class. The strike wave has either petered out entirely in the case of Network Rail, the post office and the teachers' unions, who all settled for below inflation pay deals, or stalled as with the junior doctors, consultants and train operating company workers deploying the same tactics of having a few days strike action months apart. This discontinuous action will not achieve a victory, or even substantial concessions from the government, and may well lead to further demoralisation amongst large sections of the union memberships.

This all begs the question of where do we go from here as a trade union movement? It isn't sufficient just to point out the deficiencies and not try to remedy the situation, so what are the possible alternatives? Many unions have broad lefts or even more than one left formation; unfortunately, these are usually solely propaganda and electoral machines, which never act independently of the trade union bureaucrats in regard to calling strikes or other industrial action, nor see their role as doing so. Their purpose is to capture the levers of power and in effect become the bureaucracy. Occasionally, there is an exceptional leader produced, like Bob Crow, who can pull the whole organisation to the left, but this is a rarity. More often, broad left candidates, if successful settle into their well-paid new positions and are scarcely different from those they replace.

The only hope of turning the unions into vehicles that even adequately defend workers, is to develop a cadre of people with a revolutionary perspective from the most militant workers. In order to hold back the increasing oppressive and rapacious capitalist attacks, rank-and-file workers with no wish to become part of the bureaucracy have to understand the role of the capitalist system, their bosses, and even their own union leaders in their oppression. It is only when there is an organisation of consciously revolutionary workers, who do not just want to win concessions (which are always temporary) from capitalism, but to replace it with a socialist system, will the cycle of bureaucrats selling out to management and the government stop. The rank-and-file when they have enough influence must be prepared to call action, including strikes, without jumping through the hoops that the anti-trade union laws impose. Imagine if tomorrow workers went on strike without any notice and without informing the bosses in advance. The effect would be electric, with no time to prepare contingency plans and organise scabs, the chances of winning the strike would be increased immensely.

Trade unionism as it stands in Britain is a part of the capitalist system. This may come as a shock to many very good trade unionists, but is sadly true. The role of unions and their leaderships, which play an intermediary role between the bosses and the workers is to avoid disputes. In effect, the union bureaucrats take the demands of the workers and moderate them until they are acceptable to the bosses. This negotiation is really just a form of haggling, and rarely, if ever, results in the workers' full demands being met. Clever bosses actually appreciate the roles unions play, because ameliorating the worst effects of capitalism, by keeping the workplace safe and wages at a reasonable level, all actually help retain workers and make them more efficient.

It is a totally different story when workers in a union develop a revolutionary consciousness. Things will only change when we as a class understand that our labour produces wealth and most of this wealth is stolen by the bosses, who after taking their cut in the form of profits (the money left after all costs are paid), usually pass the rest of it to the shareholders who sit at home never breaking sweat. I truly believe that when a critical mass of workers understands, even in this simplified form, their own exploitation, that trade unions can be transformed into fighting organisations that can help bring about a transition to socialism. I am not suggesting that this can be done in isolation divorced from a larger socialist movement, but neither can, nor should, the importance of the actual place the exploitation takes place, i.e., the workplace be diminished.

Given my experience, which is by no means all-encompass-
ing, of the trade unions and the British left, I have been pon-
dering some of the most obvious problems, and want to start
a discussion amongst workers as to the possible solutions.
Why are the left failing to make a necessary impact on the
council estates and the private tenants who are paying extortionate rates to landlords? Why are we becoming increasingly
irrelevant to the working-class, the poor and the oppressed
when we should be making incredible inroads? I also want
to reach out to those who are genuine left-wingers, who want
to debate my proposed solutions, to challenge, reject or re-
fine them, and in so doing to create mechanisms where we
can empower our class to throw off its oppression, and bring
about a socialist society that will benefit not a tiny elite, but
humanity in its entirety.

It has become a trend in much of the left to minimise the
role of the working-class and its historic role in overthrowing capitalism and replacing it with a socialist society, by
pushing identity politics as an alternative. Identity politics
rightly recognises that people of colour, women, LGBT, and
other minorities are more oppressed under capitalism than
white males. True proponents of intersectionality recognise
that if a woman is working-class, black and gay, then she will
almost without exception be treated worse because she is a
woman, because she is black, because she is working-class
and because she is gay. Any Marxist would accept this analysis. The problem arises when we have bourgeois identity

politics which claims to be Marxist, but in reality, is the polar opposite, playing down the class element of oppression, the most fundamental element in the capitalist system, and playing up the other elements. In effect, the proponents of this type of identity politics are saying if only LGBT, black people, and women, all had equality under capitalism, then things would be fine. Capitalism is very capable of assimilating women, working-class people, people of colour and LGBT people into the system, and even allowing them positions of privilege in it, but this in no way challenges the system itself. The mechanics of exploitation, where workers are robbed of the wealth they produce are still intact. What capitalism cannot do is assimilate the whole working-class, giving us equal rights, because once we start receiving the full amount of wealth that we create, the system collapses, the bosses and shareholders are robbed of their source of income and their privileged positions disappear.

To rebuild a politically conscious rank-and-file, grass roots organisations capable of transforming the unions from partners in capitalism to fighting organisations of the working- class, there needs to be a reorientation back to the fundamentals of class politics, especially at the point of exploitation, the workplace. This is not to ignore or downplay racism, sexism, or homophobia, and how capitalism has used these to divide the working-class, but rather to recognise that to achieve real equality, there must be a totally different form of society, based not on division and exploitation, but on mutual cooperation that benefits everyone. In a nutshell, true equality is impossible under capitalism, a system that's very basis is exploitation, and can only be achieved under a socialist structure. This lessons of the failure of the recent struggles are absolutely essential now, because, although the strike wave of 2022-23 is much diminished, and could well fail, it is important not to repeat the same mistakes. Unfortunately, to begin reconstruction of a revolutionary left, we must start from the point that much of the left is a complete failure. Those who use Marxist language, but in reality promote identity politics to the detriment of class politics, must be recognised for what they are – left liberals and not socialists.

Socialists start from the point of bringing people together to tackle their economic problems and the system that creates those problems in a collective way. Left liberal identity politicians do the opposite, they promote division and individualism, ignoring the material needs of the working-class, the thing that can bring class unity, and deliberately concentrating on differences. The effects of the abandonment of workers who were previously the bedrock of left parties by those self-same parties has opened up a space that the extreme right and fascist parties are exploiting all over Europe, and indeed the world. The rise of Trump can in part be explained by the perceived abandonment of white working-class Americans by the Democrats in favour of the "rainbow coalition" voters, who are appealed to because of their identities and not their class.

The right and the extreme right have no answer to workers problems; in reality, they pursue extreme neo-liberal policies, which further impoverish workers. The big difference of course is that the far right deliberately scapegoat ethnic or religious minorities, asylum seekers, and anyone else that they can use to distract people from the real culprit – the capitalist system. Governments that up to recently could have been described as centre right are increasingly adopting far right methods. Take, for example, Britain's policy of sending asylum seekers to Rwanda, or putting them on barges, or the American Republican Trump-led Government whipping up hysteria against Mexicans and promising to build a wall with Mexico the entire length of the border. These would have been unacceptable in the political mainstream a decade earlier. The right stealing the clothes off the far right will inevitably lead to an increase in racism and racist attacks, and in its current state, the left can offer very little resistance. It also helps legitimise far right ideas and has seen social democratic parties like Britain's Labour Party increasingly taking a far harder line on asylum seekers, dragging the whole debate to the right.

To stop the drift to the right, we of the left must immediately start reorientating ourselves towards the working-class, not some idealised leftie version of what workers should be, but rather the consciousness and material reality that workers currently have. We must make ourselves relevant to everyone in the working-class by pursuing policies that will materially benefit their lives. We must start arguing not just for a massive redistribution of wealth in Britain, but worldwide. We must drive home the fact that combatting climate change should produce millions of well-paid, skilled, unionised jobs for workers. We must rebuild pride in our class and raise aspirations, not just of individuals, but collectively. We must convince our children and grandchildren that it is not just nobler to rise with our class and not out of it, but it is the only way to ensure progress for everyone like us. There is no room for timidity: another Tory Party wearing red rosettes and calling themselves Labour, even if they are elected will not be in power, as they will be hostage to big business, multinationals, and their lapdogs in the press. Not only will this be disastrous for workers, but unless a clear pro-worker, green agenda is immediately implemented, it is not an exaggeration to say that the fate of billions of people depends on it.

43 CAPITALISM ISN'T WORKING

We just need to look at the capitalists' institutions own figures to see the institutional depravity of the system. It is necessary of course to point this out, but that will not in itself bring about any change whilst the capitalists use their astronomical wealth to control the media and create a perceived reality where questioning the status quo will result in people being labelled "extremists", and probably suffering financially in being denied jobs, and possibly losing their liberty if they decide to protest in a meaningful way that costs the system money. When 23 billionaires own as much as half the world's population, capitalism demonstrably is not working for the vast majority of people.

Whilst the left is in disarray, the contradictions in capitalism are becoming ever more apparent. We have a system where a tiny minority of the world's population controls ever greater percentages of the world's wealth. In the two years from 2020 to 2022, the richest 1 percent of the world's population took for itself forty-two trillion dollars, which amounted to around two-thirds of all new wealth created in that period. The other 99% of the world's population were left to share out the remainder. Of course, the remaining third was not shared equally, but with the bottom fifty percent receiving a miniscule amount, meaning millions more people worldwide are being pushed into poverty.

In 2021, Credit Suisse put together a pyramid that demonstrated how the world's wealth is distributed. This is not up to date, as the two years that came after made things even worse, but it does serve as a good guide to the horrific wealth inequalities we are dealing with as a planet. For the purposes of constructing the pyramid, people's personal assets were calculated as net worth. It found that 53.2% of the world's adult population, around 2.818 billion people have wealth below 10,000 U.S. dollars. That the next rung from the bottom, consisting of 33.8% of the world's population, roughly 1.791 billion adults have wealth totalling between 10,000 and 100,000 U.S. dollars. 627 million people have wealth amounting to between 100,000 – 1,000,000 U.S. dollars, that's 11.8% of the world's population. Then 1.2 % of adult population, nearly 62.5 million people, have wealth over 1,000,000 U.S. dollars.

In other words, half of the world's net wealth belongs to the top 1% of the world's population. It is incredible to think that this could be tolerated, but the unequal distribution doesn't stop there. The top 10% of people control 85% of the world's wealth, while the bottom 90% have only 15% between them. This means that the poorest 70% of people in the world share a tiny 3% of its wealth, while the combined top 30% richest people have a massive 97% of the wealth. Forecasts for the coming few years indicate a growth in wealth inequalities exacerbated by high inflation rates, especially in food prices, which hit the poor disproportionately hard. When 23 billionaires own as much as half the world's population, and the access to this information is more readily available than before, what possible excuse has the left got for not making historic advances politically?

In the diagram (figure 1) below showing the distribution on a chart, you can see that not until we reach the position of 50% of the world's entire population does their combined wealth even start visibly registering, whilst the top 0.1 percent have so much wealth that they are literally off the chart.

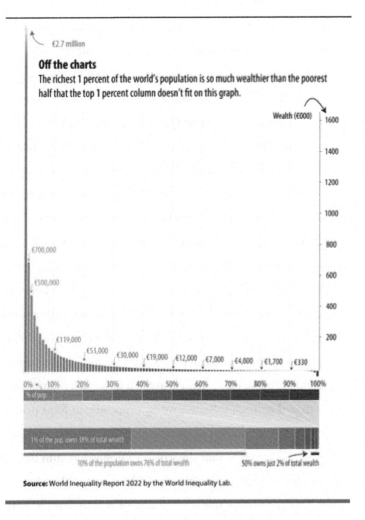

Figure 1: World inequality report 2022

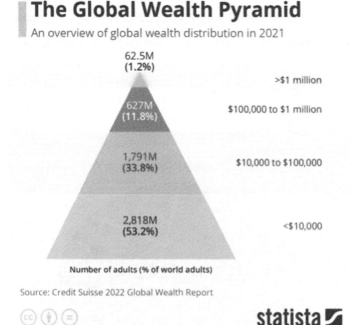

Figure 2: Global wealth pyramid 2021

The increasing concentration of the world's wealth in fewer and fewer hands and the corresponding loss felt by half the world's poorest, has plunged tens of millions into poverty. It is unsurprising that countries also have massive differences in the percentage of the world's wealth that they hold. Although it cannot be said that poverty is completely relative, there is a big difference between being poor in the global north and being poor in the global south. This inequality between nations and regions, coupled with climate change is driving mass migration that will only increase as the effects of global warming increase and poorer nations lack the resources to deal with the results. The diagram below from 2019 gives an indication of the appalling wealth dipartites between the richest and poorest nations. The situation has further deteriorated since the drawing was produced. The United States and China between them control nearly as much of the world's wealth as every other country combined.

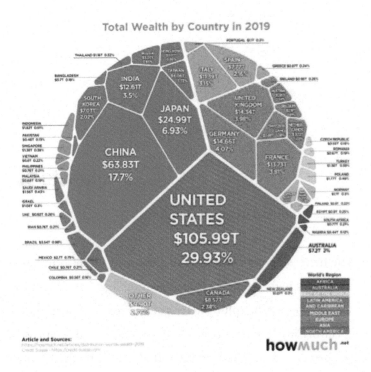

Figure 3: Total wealth by country 2019

Those of us who believe we are on the left must ask the million-dollar questions, how is it possible then when the capitalism system is not only unquestionably creating gross wealth inequalities between nations, and between the wealthy and poor within nations that we are unable to explain this to the vast majority of workers? Why when people are seeing their living standards plummet, are they looking to the extreme right for solutions and not the left? The harsh answer is that through its abandonment of class politics, most of what identifies as the left has made itself irrelevant to whole swathes of workers, as they do not offer solutions that will materially benefit the working-class. We need to address this issue immediately.

Another undeniable inequality in every country is in how much women are paid compared to men. Advanced capitalist countries are no exceptions with woman regularly earning around 20 percent, in the UK it's an astonishing 17.5%, less than men for work of similar value. Globally women are often trapped in low wage, low skilled jobs, resulting from patriarchal gender stereotyping. In addition, women often are solely or disproportionately responsible for unpaid work such as childcare and domestic chores.

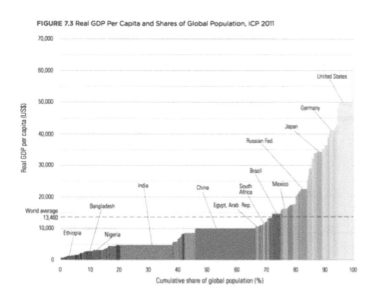

FIGURE 7.3 Real GDP Per Capita and Shares of Global Population, ICP 2011

Chidi King, Director of the Equality Department of the International Trade Union Confederation (ITUC), has described how women's role as workers is often "seen as subsidiary or supplementary to their principal role of 'homemakers'".

Women who are in employment on average still do two and a half times more housework than men. This includes caring for children and the elderly. World-wide, women are often forced to take up jobs in ununionized informal work which further erodes their earning potential, with no holiday sick pay, pensions or maternity benefits. Discrimination in pay increases with the number of children a woman has, with few companies offering flexible working, and many mothers losing out on promotion opportunities because of childcare responsibilities.

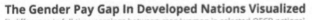

The Gender Pay Gap In Developed Nations Visualized
% difference in full-time earnings between men/women in selected OECD nations'

Country	%
South Korea	36.6%
Japan	26.6%
Netherlands	20.5%
Turkey	20.1%
Canada	19.2%
Australia	18.0%
United States	17.9%
United Kingdom	17.5%
Sweden	15.1%
France	13.4%
Germany	12.8%
Ireland	11.6%
Italy	11.1%
Spain	8.6%
New Zealand	5.6%

*as a % of the earnings of men, latest available year
@StatistaCharts   Source: OECD

statista

The gender pay gap can also be caused by a lack of programmes to support women's return to work after time out of the labour market for maternity leave, and the lack of gender responsive public services like affordable childcare so women can go back to work if they choose.

Tackling the gender pay gap must be an absolute priority for socialists, not just ensuring women are equally paid, but that men and government all play far greater roles in childcare that removes the burden from women's shoulders.

44 SYSTEM CHANGE NOT CLIMATE CHANGE

As wealth distribution goes increasingly in favour of the rich, the profit dynamic that is the principle of capitalism is destroying the planet. Once again, I have to ask myself why the established left have not made political gains from such an obvious truth which could put us in a position to reverse it. If we cannot convince people to take action that will avert incredible danger and possible death to themselves, and certainly their children and grandchildren, then what is the point of the left in its current form?

To avoid any doubt, I am putting China firmly within the capitalist camp. It is best described as state capitalism, that is state directed and planned capitalist growth. The main differences from "free market capitalism" is the transparent role of the state in encouraging the nation's capitalist expansion both internally and internationally. The other difference of course is that although many Chinese capitalists have become obscenely rich, the state maintains a controlling interest and takes a large percentage of the profits for its own use, rather than the capitalist pocketing the lot. There are similarities with mercantilism where, for example, the young USA very effectively supported its own nascent capitalists through investment and tariffs on foreign goods, but also differences in the control and use of profits, which in China remain far more in control of the state. The left must seize upon the issues of the increasing relative and real poverty of the working-class and poor worldwide and the fact that we are hurtling towards climate disaster, offering solutions to the vast majority of humanity that will benefit us.

In order to function effectively capitalism demands continuous economic growth, which requires, more commodities (goods) and services. The profit motive, the theft of the workers' labour power, to supply more wealth to companies and their shareholders means goods must be produced as cheaply as possible and workers' wages suppressed as much as possible. Capitalism operates on a global basis, and its need for ever increasing economic growth has meant its expansion into new areas – this can be different countries, regions or within countries, by privatising previously public services to allow the capitalists to make money off these too. Not only must capitalism produce more goods and services, but it must also convince people (consumers) that they need these goods and therefore purchase them. This implantation in people's minds of the need for commodities is carried out by the advertising industry which costs nearly 800 billion US dollars worldwide.

There is near unanimity amongst scientists that climate change is being driven by humans, the only exception being cranks paid mostly by energy companies to downplay the damage. Fossil fuels used to power industry lead to increases in greenhouse gases, amongst them carbon dioxide. These gasses only began to be released in such dangerous volumes from 1760-1850, which marked the beginning of the industrial revolution and the birth of capitalism. Progressive scholars recognize the serious damage that results from a global capitalist drive. In the anarchy of a "free market", where private companies compete with each other in the race for profit, it is inevitable that more fossil fuels will be used to increase production and global temperatures will rise as a result. Alternatives to fossil fuels have not been adequately developed as they do not yield the immediate short-term high profit rates that can be made in oil and gas. In a system where successful companies make the most profit, it is ludicrous to think that environmental concerns will ever trump the need to make money with individual companies or capitalism collectively. The tragedy of the situation is that most intelligent people, including the C.E.O.s and boards of most companies, recognise exactly where this dynamic is leading, namely a climate crisis and catastrophe; but because capitalism demands expansion and the profits that ensue, they cannot hit the breaks on the speeding juggernaut.

As has been shown in the previous chapter, wealth inequalities are not being reduced by the expansion of capitalism and the untold profits it produces, but rather make the rich comparatively richer and the poor comparatively poorer. Inflation since 2020 has meant that the poor have not just lost out comparatively, but in real terms, as wages have not kept pace with inflation. So, although the poor do not benefit from the rapacious capitalist system, they bear the brunt of the need for continual growth to feed profits. This is most apparent in the global south where climate change is producing record temperatures and leading to a lack of resources such as water and food. The capitalist system, by its very nature, has produced a toxic cycle of continuous economic growth demanding more power sources supplied to fossil fuels, leading to climate change which is killing people (with millions more at risk), making regions uninhabitable, driving mass immigration, and creating an ever more unequal distribution of wealth.

There is absolutely no way that the free market, whose purpose is making a profit, will ever self-regulate to such a degree that climate change will be stopped or even seriously mitigated. Only immediate and massive government intervention is capable of changing this toxic situation, and offers a chance of preventing billions from dying from the effects of climate change. We must beware of the trojan horse of our "carbon footprint", which was a concept invented by the oil companies to distract people from the companys' destruction of the environment. This seeks to delegate the responsibility for the planet's destruction onto individuals and away from the real culprits: the power companies themselves. It is abundantly clear that even if we all recycled and took more walks, the unavailability of cheap reliable public transport and green sources of heating fuel, means that we will continue to rely upon cars to travel and fossil fuels to heat our homes. The need for massive government intervention to immediately cut back on fossil fuels and invest in developing green alternatives, as well as the provision of cheap public transport to enable a sharp reduction in car use, has never been so blatantly obvious.

It is a shocking statistic to cite, but when the richest 10% in the world produce over 35% of greenhouse gases, and the poorest 50% only produce 15% of emissions, it is clear that the developed capitalist countries in the vanguard of technological advances are the culprits responsible for global warming, climate change, and the death, misery and poverty that results. Whilst Africa and Asia are undeniably bearing the brunt of climate change, Europe and North America are not immune. Europe has seen record temperatures in Portugal, Greece, Spain, Italy, and other countries, causing huge wildfires that have destroyed thousands of properties and killed scores of people. Simultaneously the USA and Canada have witnessed wildfires in some places and mass floods in others. So, although the global south is undoubtedly suffering disproportionately from climate change, the main perpetrators in the global north are not immune.

The world's top five CO_2-producing countries in 2020 were China, the United States, India, Russia, and Japan in that order. China is the biggest carbon dioxide emitter, with 10,668 million metric tons measured in 2020. This is largely down to China's reliance on fossil fuels. Over half of China's energy production comes from burning coal, which emits massive amounts of carbon dioxide. The United States emitted 4,713 million metric tons of total carbon dioxide. This came mainly from power plants using oil and coal, and transport heavily based on road haulage, aviation, and private car use. US industry is also heavily reliant on fossil fuels. India produced 2,442 million metric tons of CO_2 emissions. Coal accounts for about 45% of the country's energy and petrol, also contributing significantly to the total. Russia emitted 1,577 million metric tons with natural gas and coal being the major contributors. Japan emitted 1,577 million metric tons with oil accounting for 40% of the country's energy production, and coal 26%. It is crystal clear that industrialised nations heavily reliant on fossil fuels are responsible for the CO_2 emissions that are the key factor in global warming.

When tackled about global poverty and the fact that millions of people literally starve to death each year, capitalists often answer that "capitalism has lifted billions out of poverty". Not only is this an erroneous argument, but it is on the premise that industrial development, and growing economies year after year is the only way that the world's poor can improve their situation. The logic of this is terrifying – imagine if countries all over the global south developed their economies to the extent of the big 5 polluters. Climate change would be massively accelerated and the catastrophic effects of this would be evident a lot sooner. It is self-evident then that capitalism has no answers. The diagram below dramatically illustrates the disproportionate contribution to global warming made by the top 5 offenders. Imagine the impact if the model of development that capitalism is pushing was adopted by every one of the world's 195 countries.

What then is the solution? If continuous growth, which is demanded for capitalism to succeed is destroying the planet, which has limited resources and is already being driven not only to the brink, but into the beginnings of environmental disaster what is the alternative? The only solution to a system that demands more and more growth, in order that the rich take an ever-greater proportion of the wealth produced, is to have a planned economy that will distribute the world's wealth far more evenly, not only across countries, but also amongst the populations of each country. This requires nothing short of a worldwide socialist system. I can imagine my political opponents choking on their caviar and champagne on reading this. The billionaires will not surrender their wealth nor the system that creates their wealth voluntarily, even if the price of them clinging onto their privileges is the death of billions of people. Their puppets in the media, the mainstream political parties, and many of those who self-identify as left, will argue that this is utopian fantasy that can never be achieved. These self-same "reasonable" people cannot see the irony in defending a system, that although they have benefited from, is already in the process of ensuring our collective destruction.

The left must seize upon the issues of the increasing relative and real terms poverty of the working-class and poor worldwide, and the fact that we are hurtling towards climate disaster. We must offer solutions to the vast majority of humanity that will benefit everyone, not just economically, but without exaggeration, show how it's a matter of life and death that capitalism must be superseded with a global socialist system.

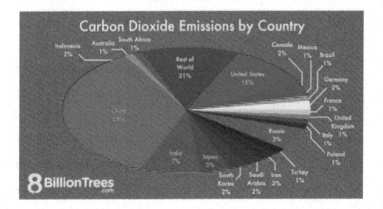

45 DON'T MENTION THE WAR

Capitalist states have always fought over markets and control of natural resources and the 21st Century is absolutely no exception to this rule. Russia's invasion of Ukraine on February 24th, 2022, is a prime example of new emerging capitalist and global forces challenging the existing hegemony of the United States and its allies.

Like it or not, the Russians see Ukraine joining NATO as an existential threat with the military alliance pushing right up to Russia's border despite the guarantee from George Bush Senior and his secretary of state, George Baker, that there would be no extension of NATO eastward (a promise broken several times). President Biden wanted to admit Ukraine to NATO in 2021, provoking the Russian invasion.

Admitting Ukraine into NATO does not just have military consequences, but economic and political ones too. In 2008, the NATO summit in Bucharest declared that Georgia and Ukraine would be allowed to join. Russia's leaders were furious. This was pointed out by the then US ambassador, who reported to Condoleezza Rice, the secretary of state that "it was the brightest of all red lines" for the Russians and a "direct challenge" to their interests and even as "the throwing down of the strategic gauntlet". France and Germany were also very concerned at the proposed move and what the repercussions could be. With Angela Merkel the German chancellor stating that from Putin's perspective, "that would be a declaration of war". Nevertheless, both France and Germany were pressured by America to agreeing that the Ukraine and should join.

The first consequence was the Russian Georgian war in 2008 — just months after the Bucharest declaration. The US was not deterred, funding the overthrow of a pro-Russian democratically elected Ukrainian government in February 2014. In response Russia seized Crimea from Ukraine and funded separatists in the Donbass region, who saw themselves as Russian, and were not prepared to accept the coup funded and organised by the west. NATO began training Ukrainian troops at a rate of around 10,000 a year for every year until the Russian invasion. In 2017, Trump once again raised the stakes with the US and its allies providing "defensive weapons" to the Kyiv regime. Joint military exercises between NATO and Ukraine took place, and in July 2021, Ukraine co-hosted a Black Sea naval exercise with ships from no less than 31 different countries. In September of the same year, Ukraine's army led "rapid Trident" with the U.S. These exercises were obviously a not too subtle message to Moscow to "keep out of the Ukraine's business or else".

Originally Ukrainian president, Zelensky, who was seen as a peacemaker with no enthusiasm for joining NATO, was elected in 2019 on a platform of cooperation with Russia. This all changed in early 2021, when he took an anti-Russian stance and demanded to join NATO. He shut down TV stations that supported Russia and arrested some high-profile Russian supporters. Biden, who also took power in January 2021, was a known hawk on Russian issues, and on June 14th, 2021, reiterated the decision made at the 2008 Bucharest Summit that Ukraine will become a member of NATO. Zelensky went to visit Biden in September 2021 where Biden once again went public in support of Ukraine's NATO membership. In November the cat was well and truly let out of the bag when the "U.S.-Ukraine Charter on Strategic Partnership" was signed committing the Ukraine to implement "deep and comprehensive reforms necessary for full integration into European and Euro-Atlantic institutions", and reaffirming the US commitment to the "2008 Bucharest Summit Declaration." In a nutshell the Ukraine had promised to make economic, political and strategic military changes that would enable it to be accepted into NATO and that would be detrimental to Russia.

In response to the perceived threat, Russia began massing troops on Ukraine's border between 2021 and February 2022. This was to try and force the US and Ukraine into backtracking. At the end of 2021, Putin wrote to Biden and Zelensky asking for guarantees that:

1. Ukraine would not join NATO.
2. No offensive weapons would be stationed near Russia's borders.
3. NATO troops and equipment would be removed from Ukraine.

Putin meanwhile made no bones about his intentions regarding the encroachment of NATO onto "the doorstep of our house". He warned that Russia would not "sit idly by" while the United States "continue to pump the current Kyiv authorities full of modern types of weapons". When the Ukrainians and the US refused to change course, the invasion was launched.

The number of Russian troops initially deployed in the invasion did not indicate a real intention to occupy the country, but rather an attempt to dislodge the Ukrainian government and perhaps install an administration far more friendly to Moscow. Fierce Ukrainian resistance, no doubt enabled by NATO training and weapons, meant that this was not achieved and humiliatingly, Russian forces were made to retreat from around Kyiv, but a year on they retained control of most of the Donbass and much of the Southern Ukraine bordering on Crimea. Over a year into the conflict there is now a grinding stalemate with neither side being able to gain much ground despite the vaunted "Ukrainian spring offensive" which made practically no progress and got bogged down in mine fields.

Socialists in my view cannot support the invasion of an independent country, neither can we support the imperialist military alliance that is NATO. There is no doubt that fascists and out-right Nazis have organised in the Ukrainian government and army. The AZOV battalion are an openly neo-Nazi part of the Ukrainian army. The coup in 2014 was spearheaded by the far right. There is also evidence of discrimination and violence towards Russian speakers in the Donbass and elsewhere, with the Russian language being derecognised by the state, Soviet war memorials destroyed, and war time fascists like Bandeira being glorified. That is not to say that the Ukraine is a fascist state, it is a state run by pro-western oligarchs where the far right have a big influence on the government. Socialists should be calling for the unity of Russian and Ukrainian workers and the overthrowing of their respective ruling classes.

Meanwhile the consequences for workers in Ukraine, Russia and worldwide are tragic. No less than 6 and a half million Ukrainians left their country at the height of the invasion and another 10 million fled the violence, but remained there. Hundreds of billions worth of economic devastation has been unleased with the Ukrainian economy needing massive western intervention to survive. A renewed Russian blockade of the Black Sea has seen grain prices soar and food inflation world-wide, with the poorest suffering hunger and even starvation. Russian workers have seen the introduction of conscription as hundreds of thousands of casualties were inflicted on their troops.

With neither Moscow nor Washington prepared to back down, the best-case scenario seems to be a long and debilitating war. In the worst case, there could be an escalation that could even turn nuclear. As capitalist powers jockey for position to dominate the world's markets, there is also the risk that the US may continue its economic aggression towards China, drawing it into a conflagration over Taiwan. Workers cannot sit by passively whilst our annihilation is planned to ensure markets and profits. Worse, we cannot side with our own exploiters and linguistically support calls for war. Rather we must campaign for peace and the abolition of the capitalist system that is threatening our destruction.

46 A PLAN OF ACTION

It will take intellectual and physical courage to take on the system and all its layers of oppression. The "left wing" careerists will not seriously challenge their paymasters, it's far easier to be a "respectable leftie" who criticises the worst aspects of the system, but who won't jeopardise their own privileged livelihoods to challenge it fundamentally. There will be no jobs in journalism or TV punditry for anyone who seeks to challenge the power, wealth, and sociopathy of our rulers. Similarly, physical courage will be needed. The elite who rules at the current time or the "ruling class" as we on the left call them, will not sit idly by as we attempt to redistribute the wealth and power that they have monopolised. They will resort to any means, coercion by the police and army, jailing protesters and banning strikes, to protect their privilege. They believe their money will protect them from the worst effects of climate change and are already buying up strips of land to fortify if the worst scenarios unfold. New Zealand is a location where already billionaires like Google's Larry Page and Pay Pal's Sam Altman have bought real estate to prepare for possible catastrophe.

Given the balance of power between the mega-rich and the rest of us, acts of collective and individual resistance will be the only possibility of redressing the current power relations. Workers, community activists and everyone under attack, must be prepared to take part in acts of civil disobedience and exercise the right to self-defence when attacked. Mass protests are preferable, but until these are possible, individuals or small groups can raise important issues like climate change by imaginative protests. Extinction Rebellion, Just Stop Oil and Greenpeace have been at the forefront of using tactics that keep humanity's survival in the papers and on our screens. They have been pilloried in the press, imprisoned, and assaulted for pointing out the obvious in a way that disrupts the profit-making of the rich and which draws media attention. In the future I believe some of these partisans may well be incarcerated, perhaps on trumped-up charges or even assassinated by state agents. If you think that this is hyperbole, look at the history of the British Government funding, arming and helping loyalist death squads to eliminate political opponents. In 2007, the police ombudsman, Nuala O'Loan, revealed how Special Branch ran loyalist terrorists, using them as informers and allowing them to commit no less than 15 murders. This collusion was with the Ulster Volunteer Force (UVF) and was just in north Belfast over a 12-year period, so is clearly just the tip of the iceberg. It was common knowledge that since the war of resistance began in the occupied 6 counties in the North of Ireland that collusion, including murder of political opponents, has been systematic and controlled by the British state.

Don't think for a second that the same oppression won't be unleashed on anyone who seriously challenges the state in Britain. Those who rule will be utterly ruthless in maintaining their astronomical privileges. The slogan of effecting change "by any means necessary" must become a rallying call for action, and not just a cliched phrase thrown about by people who've never risked anything, let alone their lives and liberty. The battle lines are currently being drawn, the only thing that we have on our side is the potential weight of numbers, as every ordinary person who does not have the money to buy huge compounds in New Zealand and fortify them, is in dire risk of extinction. We need to mobilise the mass of people who currently feel disempowered and unable to change our collective fate. We must do this with every tool in our box, to combat the inevitable wrath of the state upon us, and preparation must begin now.

In a battle where the forces are so uneven, the asymmetry dictates that certain strategies and tactics should be employed. So, if we set our objective as stopping climate any way we can, we need to analyse continuously how this can be achieved.

We have to understand that our opponents in the elite hold most of the cards, that they will deploy all the forces of the state including the police, army, prisons and the media against us, demonising whatever actions we take to resist them and criminalising peaceful protest in order to achieve this. Even an unpopular government with an unpopular leader has massive resources to manipulate public opinion and turn people whose very survival depends on stopping climate change against the very activists who are trying to stop it.

Given the massive imbalances in power between protesters and the government, careful planning of each action whether it be protest, demonstration or a march, needs to take place. Just as importantly, an honest reflection on what was successful, what can be improved and what was plainly counterproductive, is essential. It is pointless to continue with tactics, however effective, if they only alienate the working-class base upon which we are seeking to build.

Once the activist is seen as "the enemy of the people" by the population itself, the task will become extremely difficult to accomplish. There are a limited number of activists who will put themselves in harm's way and if they are alienated from the mass of the population, they will become easy targets for the state to pick off. If it gets to the stage where most working-class people would rather inform on activists than listen to their arguments, then it's very difficult indeed to effect change.

There does however need to be a build-up, and if possible, increase in pressure upon the state. Actions need to take place strategically, but also as often as can be maintained. The government must never be allowed to think that they have the time to recuperate, rest, and plan their next move. Protests must involve, if at all possible, participation by local people, as outsiders coming in, especially if their actions are disruptive to everyday lives, will not be viewed kindly by working-class communities. The idea of highly educated middle-class self-appointed saviours preaching to workers, and taking actions that will alienate them is quite frankly a disastrous one. Time must be taken to build links with communities, through consistent leafleting, social media work, and local meetings, not just to convince them of a pre-planned strategy, but to open up a dialogue where workers' experiences and ideas are as valid as those of the activists in devising successful strategies of resistance.

It is absolutely essential that workers are empowered and not seen as mere pawns, or at best, low-level supporters for opposing climate change. Sometimes activists, especially from the middle-class have forgotten or have never experienced the terror or embarrassment that handing out a leaflet, or moreover engaging in a conversation, with someone who may well be hostile, entails. This is alien territory for the average worker, but once they have built up their confidence, they more often than not, are far more effective in convincing other workers of the validity of their cause and recruiting new forces to it. Council estates need to become fortresses where people can see clearly how their own oppression and economic circumstances are not just bad luck but are a systemic part of the capitalist system. We need to empower workers to draw the conclusions that they will suffer much greater distress as climate change accelerates and motivate themselves to challenge and ultimately replace the system that is the cause of their distress.

In the first instance, the spreading of the message is very important and environmental activists have been incredibly successful in keeping the issues in the mainstream press. Of course, the press, being the paid lackeys of elite have been scathing in their attacks on activists, sparing no slander and spreading disinformation to tarnish the opponents of their pay masters. There does, however, need to be a progression from merely awareness raising and occasional disruption, into empowering workers to take action themselves, by refusing to take part in projects that will contribute to climate change and by striking against them.

The ultimate goal would be a general strike, not just in one country, but worldwide, in order to not just stop climate change but to actually definitively change the system where the destruction of the environment is inevitable. This may seem like pie in the sky but there is a long and proud history of workers acting for the environment. Green bans were first introduced in the 1970s by the New South Wales (BLF) Building Labourers Federation. These bans, which were refusals to work, were always done after consulting with the local communities involved and securing their support. The first ban was at Kelly's Bush, the last remaining bushland that wasn't built on in Hunters Hill, a suburb of Sydney. A residents group made up mainly of women went to the BLF after fruitless appeals to the council, the local mayor and even the Premier of New South Wales. Whilst the politicians sided with the building companies, the BLF backed the residents. At a public meeting that saw over 600 residents attend, the BLF were asked to instigate the ban and agreed to put the environment before the building companies' profits. The building boss, Jennings, threatened to use scab labour to break the strike and ensure that the development took place. The BLF retaliated by saying that its members would go on strike at other Jennings sites if scabs were used. The attempt at union busting by the employers backfired when union members downed tools as several sites and forced the company to backtrack on its plans to develop Kelly's Bush.

Union spokespeople pointed out that rather than destroy the environment for high-end profiteering projects, they wanted to build hospitals, "schools, other public utilities, high-quality flats, units, and houses, provided they are designed with adequate concern for the environment". This was ground-breaking stuff at the time. Builders were saying yes, of course we want to work and have jobs, but we want to use our skills to benefit working-class people and protect the environment, not to just make massive profits for the employers and sod everyone else. As the union spokesperson succinctly put it "The environmental interests of three million people are at stake and cannot be left to developers and building employers whose main concern is making profit". This trailblazing action saw the BLF develop from an organisation that looked after workers' rights into an organisation that prioritised the fundamental rights of working-class communities to live in a decent environment. Various green bans were called until 1975, when a coalition of a Labour Government, the Communist Party of Australia which was very influential in the wider union movement, and the employers, conspired to de-register the New south Wales BLF from the Arbitration Commission. This attempt to smash the most militant section of the union didn't work, as other unions in the region refused to recruit and represent BLF members. Rather than compromise through the arbitration committee the BLF were winning disputes on the ground around green issues, publicising environmental issues and gaining public support outside the residents directly affected. The government and its media lackeys went into overdrive accusing the union of being undemocratic and seeking to "run the country".

The end of the New South Wales branch was brought about when economic conditions changed and the building boom ended in 1975. The bosses and union bureaucrats went to the federal level forming a new "federal branch" to replace the NSW branch. This allowed the employers to sack and blacklist the NSW militants with complicity from union leaders who did nothing to combat the dismissals.

Striking on environmental issues is by no means confined to Australia. 1976 saw British builders ban asbestos at the Barbican at the massive Centre site in London run by Laing. Over 500 UCATT members went on strike for two weeks. Their demands were a complete asbestos ban to protect not only the workers, "but the people who move in as well". Unfortunately, the leadership bureaucrats did not back the ban, but this didn't stop Camden Direct Labour Organisation refusing to work with it. When the ban caught on in several other building sites, Laing were defeated and had to concede, and this is why the Barbican has always been asbestos free. Asbestos was finally banned in 1999, so workers were decades ahead of government and safety "experts".

Nor is the action confined to the 1970s. Environmental campaign group Greenpeace sought to stop the dumping of nuclear waste into the sea and tried to build alliances with the trade unions to achieve this. The union in question, the National Union of Seamen (N.U.S.), now a part of the RMT, and despite opposition from his own executive members, the General Secretary Jim Slater eventually convinced them to back sailors who refused to dump extremely dangerous and toxic radioactive waste into the oceans. He was able to convince the union executive to adopt a policy of non-cooperation and seek cross-union support. In 1983 the union went further advocating that all transport unions banned the moving of nuclear waste. In June the transport unions, NUR, ASLEF and the TGWU formally backed a boycott of dumping nuclear waste, leading the Conservative government into a humiliat-ing climbdown and having to ban the practice entirely.

It may come as a complete shock to readers to find out that some of the most overt and successful mobilisation of work-ers in defence of the planet are very recent. These of course are given minimum publicity and are completely downplayed by states and internationally. 2019 was an historic year, the previous 12 months had seen record temperatures and an explicit warning by the Intergovernmental Panel of Climate change (IPCC) concluded that humanity had only 12 years left to limit global warming to 1.5°C above pre-industrial levels, or an environmental catastrophe would inevitably result.

In response hundreds of thousands of school students worldwide went on strike. Swedish schoolgirl, Greta Thun-berg was a leader of the movement that was both amazingly effective in gaining publicity and encouragingly showed that young people were far from the apathetic apolitical creatures that the mainstream media portrayed them as. Extinction Re-bellion activists who took part in an "uprising", closing down much of central London by civil disobedience such as occupa-tions and sit-down protests.

The high point so far is undoubtedly the Global Climate Strike, which took place from 20th to 27th September 2019. This saw a massive seven million protesters and strikers demand an "end to fossil fuel to avoid climate breakdown". This represents a huge leap in consciousness. Trade union in-volvement was important with the International Trade Union Confederation (ITUC) backing the action and encouraging its 200 million members to take part. Britain had over 200 rallies, with the TUC (amazingly given their record of cowardice) backing a half hour action call. I am proud to say that the RMT actively organised its members to attend rallies; unfortunately, it did not break the law for calling strikes which may have been a game changer. Nevertheless, over 100,000 people turned out to a rally in central London. Some councils including Camden backed the campaign declaring "a climate emergency" and encouraging its workers to attend. This action was mirrored world-wide.

There is clear and recent precedent for workers acting in their own interests and to benefit the planet and this should be the model we are aiming for today. We must organise in the workplaces and the communities, not just to spread knowledge, but with the concrete aim of sparking action that will stop climate change. As this process unfolds, we need to continually make the link that capitalism, driven by the bottom line, the need to make profit, is unable to morph into a system that can meet these needs, and therefore is no longer a system that we can allow to dominate how everyone behaves on this planet. The workplaces and communities must become the bastions of environmental socialism, because the workers who have no chance of avoiding climate disaster by spending huge sums of money in building huge, fortified compounds have the most to lose, unless an immediate and drastic change is made. We must quickly reach a situation where a coalition of unions, residents associations and environmental activist groups come together in a coalition that not only defends itself when attacked, but takes the battle to the enemy in different forms, but with a unity of purpose.

To reach a position where we can seriously challenge the state, environmental socialists must begin orientating their activity towards the working-class as it exists, and not in an idealised form. We must recognise that although people are aware of the impending tragedy, they simultaneously believe that they are powerless to prevent it. Work in unions and the communities is essential, using examples of how the green bans were effective, we can empower workers, pointing out that when we are organised and politically aware we can achieve incredible things. Whenever council flats are scheduled for demolition, socially cleansing local working-class people to allow building companies to make massive profits from selling new properties to the middle classes, activists need to be instrumental, agitating in the unions and community groups to stop it. Gentrification of working-class areas must be one of the main battlefields where environments activists can build a base. A few successes will not only empower those involved directly in the actions, but will inspire resistance in other working-class communities, all the while emphasising the principle that workers acting in their own interest, and demanding a system where decisions are not based on profit margins, is the only possible salvation for humanity. Successful campaigns need to help support the less experienced seeking not to colonise and control new groups, but to give advice, ideas and resources that are necessary to win, but most importantly let local people take the lead, and in so doing get a sense of their own power. Eventually if we carry out systematic work, in union after union, estate after estate, we will be able to challenge the hegemony of the ruling class and be in a position to oppose its instruments of oppression like the police, army and the press. Only the working-class has both an obvious and urgent need to stop climate change and take down the capitalist system that is causing it, and only the working-class through fulfilling its historic mission to bring about a worldwide socialist society can achieve both these critical objectives. It literally is either "socialism or extinction".

47 YOU THOUGHT IT WAS ALL OVER, WELL IT IS NOW

I have often been asked why as an Irish Republican have, I spent so much of my life fighting for English people. On the face of it it's a fair question, surely Irish Republicans should devote their whole time to achieving Irish independence. The answer as far as I'm concerned anyway is that socialism is an international philosophy. My nationality is Irish, but I have got far more in common with English working-class people than I have with Irish millionaires. The Irish republic which I long for is a socialist republic, not a 32-county capitalist neo colony. I fight for workers' rights in Britain because I live there, and am in a way an Irishman who is also part of the British working-class, and I see it as my duty to aid workers no matter what their nationality is against the common enemy, the British and indeed the international ruling class. If socialism is achieved in Britain, it will be much easier to achieve in Ireland and vice versa. As James Connolly pointed out, it is pointless taking down the union jack and replacing it with a tricolour if the capitalist system of exploitation remains and we don't set about creating a socialist society. I honestly believe that a planned socialist world is now the only possible salvation for humanity.

I have spent the past year since I resigned from the RMT by returning to university and getting a qualification in teaching in further education. I had to take a year-long teaching degree level course to qualify myself to teach adults. I started my educational journey as an adult in my local further education college in East Ham, and I hope that I can inspire people like I was inspired by my lecturer, John Batt. My core values remain the same and I think that the coming decade will be absolutely vital to our existence on this planet. I want to help students shake off all the indoctrination and conditioning that much of the education system is designed to instil in them. I want my students to be able to think critically and to ask why someone is telling them something, the timing of the message, and what reaction the messenger wants to provoke. This is the first step in challenging all the messages, obvious and subliminal that the ruling class in a capitalist society send out continuously in the education system, in the media and in every institution of the state. The climate crisis and the disproportionately terrible effect that it will have on working-class people will cause people to question and look for answers. The far right will be vying for the ears of workers to pour poison into them, turning worker against worker on grounds of race, sex, sexuality, religion and gender. They do this ultimately to protect the power wealth and privilege of the super-rich who fund them. We, on the left, must be in a position to counter this, in the workplace, in the community and in the educational system. I hope to play a part in this struggle in any capacity that I can.

I have applied for hundreds of jobs in both education and on the railway, together with various other jobs that have come up. I have had absolutely no success and am not getting to the interview stage except on a few isolated occasions. I think that I am once again being blacklisted for my political beliefs and trade union activities – there is always a price for non-conformity. On the bright side, I have had a lot of time to spend time with my family and friends, to think, to read new things and to write down my ideas. I hope that you have enjoyed reading this book or at least parts of it. My experiences have led me to forming the beliefs that I have today. I think many people of my generation from the North of Ireland share many, if not all of my experiences, and I would love to hear of these, both the similarities and differences.

I hope my writing has opened up a space for discussion and debate on how we can prevent human extinction by avoiding climate catastrophe, and also create a far more equal society on a global and national basis. I think socialism and saving the planet are completely and utterly intertwined. We either have a global system that gives every person a decent standard of life, or we fall into an abyss pushed by the need for increasing industrialisation and competition for profit. Capitalism, with its anarchic rule of the market and insatiable desire for profit at all costs, has pushed us to the brink of the abyss, only through the adoption of cooperative, socialist planning for a better world can we walk away from the impending disaster. We have a choice of either a planned socialist world acknowledging that we have limited resources and living accordingly, or continuing the road to destruction to provide nauseatingly large profits for a few. The choice is stark. It is socialism or extinction, choose wisely, your life and that of your children depend on it.